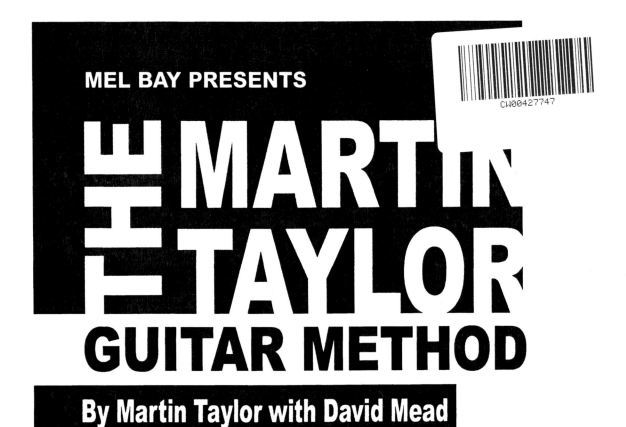

MEL BAY PRESENTS

THE MARTIN TAYLOR GUITAR METHOD

By Martin Taylor with David Mead

CD CONTENTS

Cover photo credits: Sarkis Boyadijan
CD produced, compiled/edited by Phil Hilborne. Mastered by Phil Hilborne.
Recorded/mixed by Phil Hilborne at WM Studios, Essex, Enland 12/2001 – 1/20...
Web/Info: www.philhilborne.com or www.philhilborne.co.uk
Equipment: Martin Taylor used a Vanden 'Artistry' Martin Taylor Signature Arch Top guitar.
Strings: Elixir. Beyer and Rode Mics. TLA Vavle Pre Amp. Lexicon and Yamaha effects.
Web/Info: www.martintaylor.com or www.davidmead.net

1 2 3 4 5 6 7 8 9 0

Visit us on the Web at www.melbay.com — E-mail us at email@melbay.com

THANKS

I'd like to thank all the musicians I've played with over the years - I've learned something from every single one of them! - Martin Taylor

EDITOR'S NOTE

Please be aware that the chord symbols in this book are below each system according to British practice.

ACKNOWLEDGEMENTS

Music examples transcribed by Guthrie Govan & David Mead
Music Typesetting Chris Francis @ Camnote, Alexander House, Forehill, Ely, Cambs CB7 4ZA UK
Photography by Carol Farnworth

CD recorded and produced by Phil Hilborne

For Ike Isaacs, with thanks and appreciation for his wisdom, guidance and friendship...

CONTENTS

Martin's Foreword

To begin this book, I thought I'd start off by talking to you a little bit about my feelings on jazz. When I began to learn to play the guitar, I didn't look at it as an academic subject at all, and still don't. To me, I was just playing music, that's all. As I developed as a musician, I continued to look at jazz in very much the same way. It's always been difficult for me to look at jazz as something you learn in a classroom and so I never teach jazz from that point of view. I believe that people can be taught the way I learned, which is by listening to the music and understanding some of its basic principles and not being hidebound by an awful lot of unnecessary information.

In many ways, learning jazz is like learning a language. The best way to learn a language fluently, obviously, is to be spoken to by your mother from birth in her native tongue. Similarly, if you grow up, as I did, with a certain kind of music, it will be easier to be fluent in that music. But it's never too late to learn and we can all become fluent in a certain language or music form by absorbing as much as possible naturally, by listening. Study should then be superimposed onto this natural aural exposure. On the rare occasions that I have taught at music schools I have a great problem because students tend to want an intellectual explanation for what I do. There isn't one. The intellect is the wrong tool for the job. It's of no use to you. To make music you must use your heart and miss out your head completely.

I sometimes find that I can talk about music far easier if I can relate it to painting, because I think of it like that. My friend and mentor Ike Isaacs always used to relate music to cooking, so I guess we're all different.

To illustrate this idea even further, walking into a pretty garden, you don't need to know the names of the plants to appreciate that they work well together. You're more concerned with the colour balance, tone and effect rather than the academic side of things.

When you perform, you're asking your audience to spend time in a pretty place, too - although arguably it's not always pretty! You're creating a landscape, an environment for them with every tune you play. It has to sound balanced and natural, and not like a lesson you've learned by rote. If you try to create something from an analytical set of principles, you might even end up not doing something because it isn't correct technically. Nothing will progress unless someone out there bends the rules occasionally.

I don't analyze anything I do: if it sounds good it is good, if it feels right, it is right.

Another thing I believe is that playing jazz has got nothing to do with playing licks – although there are jazz licks, of course. But the best players are actually composing when they take a solo – not just stringing licks together.

A solo may start off being subdued, but the player will work and work on it so that it's always on the incline creatively. It doesn't have to get busier or faster necessarily, but it must develop. You shouldn't start off blisteringly and have nothing left to say immediately afterwards – like telling the punchline before the joke. You have to spend time feeling your way because when you start playing you don't really know what you're going to do; you just ease your way in and find something there to build upon.

Another thing I always tell people is that there are no mistakes – only opportunities. You may play something you didn't mean to play, but you can always use it to your advantage by letting it take you in a new direction.

So don't get too concerned with the idea of which scale is politically correct over each chord, or even which chord supports a particular melody note the best – it's much more important that you listen to as much jazz playing as possible and try to absorb the ideas played by all the great musicians out there. Aim to play the music that's inside your head, not somebody else's.

Martin Taylor
West Scotland
Autumn 2002

David's Foreword

At the end of the 1950s, Miles Davis went on record saying that he thought that the bop era had brought about a situation where many jazz musicians were overly concerned with improvising on chords, harmonically, as opposed to melodically. His album, Kinda Blue, reflected his desire to redirect jazz back to its melodic roots and remove the dominance of harmonic concerns. What he was perhaps seeing was the beginnings of a jazz academia; something that would continue to grow over the ensuing years.

When jazz became respectable enough for people to teach it formally, it suffered from the same basic syndromes that apply every time an art form is taught like a science. Students become hidebound with formulae, applied methodology and other scholastic paraphernalia, losing sight of the fact that melody is very likely the one thing that attracted us all to our chosen instruments in the first place.

It's become commonplace to see jazz students taking a headlong leap into a standard like it was some kind of jazz obstacle course that can be beaten by scale theory. The main problem is that these guerrilla tactics always sound wrong; too planned, contrived and not in keeping with the spirit of the music at all.

The teacher is faced with one basic paradox: people need rules. Rules make a subject like music less scary because there's a method to learning it, an infrastructure to rely upon. But nothing as free spirited as jazz can be tied down to something as mundane as a method book. Jazz is more organic than that.

From a student's point of view, too, it's very difficult to grasp something when it's been broken down into its smallest component parts. Can an automobile be recognized from its smallest single component? The same is true of music; the 'bigger picture' that we all seek is an elusive creature and true enlightenment always seems to be a long way off.

When Martin and I started talking about this tutor, we both wanted to avoid the norm of the highly stylized rule book. We wanted to reintroduce a lot of the older values of music study, encourage listening and promoting self-discovery as the path towards 'enlightenment'.

What you have before you now represents a rare glimpse into the workings of a very singular musician's mind. All the answers are here, the rest is up to you.

David Mead
Bath
Autumn 2002

INTRODUCTION

This guitar method is not aimed at the absolute beginner. To get the most from it, you will need a knowledge of basic music theory and harmony and have already developed many of the basic skills necessary for playing.

You may, however, be fairly new to playing jazz, and if this is the case and you are not used to the concept of soloing in jazz then you're probably aware that there tends to be a lot of 'outside playing' going on. That is, jazz players tend to use a lot of chromatic notes or scale 'extensions' when they play. These would be defined as sharp or flat 9ths, flat 5ths and so on and jazz students get themselves into all sorts of bother by trying to include this kind of harmonic information in their playing before they really know what to do with it. It's a matter of resolution - these notes are dissonant in quality and have to be resolved correctly otherwise everything comes out sounding unbalanced and 'wrong'.

These chromatic, non-scale, tones are the ones that give this style of music its principle melodic signature. At one point in jazz's history, musicians used to stick pretty much within the framework of the chord arrangement, using arpeggios as their principal source for improvisation. To illustrate this for yourself, take the first four chords of any jazz standard and arpeggiate them over the bass line and you should be able to hear how this system worked. Other scale tones were included along the way, of course, just to add interest, but everything remained diatonic, or faithful to the key of the piece. The use of notes from outside of the scale was pioneered by the be-bop jazzers of the 30s and 40s, the most popular exponent of which was undoubtedly the saxophonist Charlie Parker. The music instantly became more tense with a constant battle between tension and resolution in solos and melody lines.

From a technical point of view, all that was happening was that chromatic tones were being used as sort of 'stepping stones' between the regular scale tones, adding splashes of dissonance along the way. If you want to illustrate this point to yourself, try playing a simple G7 chord four to the bar and slide into it from a G♭7 just before the first beat of the bar. It doesn't sound ugly or out of place, does it? All that's going on with the use of chromatic tones in jazz is that precise concept expanded somewhat.

I've said before that I don't like analyzing jazz too much. When in a playing context, the musician's ear is his first line of defense, having been 'programmed' by years of listening and practice to recognize points of tension and release within a melodic line. It becomes familiar and natural to him in the same way and artist's eye becomes trained to work with colour. I believe this kind of training has to be ear based and relies upon an awful lot of research on behalf of the student. This doesn't mean hours of study pouring over a text book; you can learn by listening to music, looking through transcriptions of solos and seeing for yourself which notes give the desired 'jazz' effect.

It's a good idea to familiarize your fingers with the chromatic scale on the fingerboard, too - more on this later; this way, your hand will be able to deal with all the slight position shifts needed to accommodate the chromatic passing notes.

Any clues?

A lot of the different music styles have adopted a kind of standard chord sequence. Take the blues for example; where would we be without the C, F, G or I IV V chord sequence? It's a thing that has become standardized and, as such, is invaluable for anyone learning to play. If you can play over basic I IV V changes in blues, you know that you can cope with a great amount of the material you'll be confronted with in that style.

You may be tempted to think that the same cannot be said for jazz. This is a music which is renowned for its non-conformist attitude towards harmony and so surely there can't be any kind of standardization here? Well, the answer is both wrong and right. Jazz does resist some 'standard' forms and isn't quite as easy to pin down as a blues or folk song. But just occasionally we come across some parallels which are beneficial to the jazz student.

It all goes back to George Gershwin and Charlie Parker, really. For some reason, Parker loved to play over the changes to Gershwin's 'I Got Rhythm' and he was probably solely responsible for that song entering the jazz repertoire in the way that it has. But you couldn't play the same song several times during a set - even the slowest audience is going to notice that. So Parker wrote a whole bundle of tunes which used the same basic chord arrangement. That way, nobody would notice and he'd get to play over his favorite set of changes several times a gig. This kind of cunning would be invisible to anything other than an audience of musicologists and so everyone was happy.

This tune enjoyed fairly humble beginnings as part of a Gershwin musical called 'Girl Crazy' during the 1930s. In all probability it would have slipped into respectable retirement, having long since hung up its dancing shoes and put away the greasepaint if it wasn't for the be-bop movement. But its chord structure crops up time and time again in real books everywhere. You still hear jazz musicians talk about 'rhythm changes' today, and what they mean is that the song is basically the chord structure of Gershwin's original, with a different 'head' on it. After all, you can copyright a tune, but not its chord structure. It's amazing what a variety of tunes share the 'I Got Rhythm' harmonic structure - even 'Meet The Flintstones' is basically 'I Got Rhythm' with a different tune.

So 'I Got Rhythm' has become one of the most important tunes - or chord arrangements, anyway - in jazz. Charlie Parker learned to play over the changes in every key, because obviously each key calls for different fingering assignments on the sax. In theory at least, this is a chore we don't have to perform as the guitar lends itself to transposition far more easily - learn a tune at the seventh fret and move it up three and voila, you've got a different key with the same essential fingering.

So, if you're going to learn just one standard, 'I Got Rhythm' would be top of the list. Search out the music and familiarize yourself with both melody and harmony. Seek out some transcriptions of solos based upon it, treat each lick you learn like a phrase in a foreign language; you're trying to build up a vocabulary in jazz by learning a few useful sentences at a time.

QUICK START JAZZ!

The biggest secret I know about playing jazz guitar is that there isn't a secret at all. It's all down to hard work, dedication and skill and always has been. There's little doubt that there are some to whom skill in music comes easier than most, but there are still hours and hours of practice and gaining experience on the bandstand to take into account at every turn.

I'm aware, too, that an awful lot of books that concern themselves with jazz try to make out that it's an arcane science, as opposed to an art form. I for one have never thought that art and science are a particularly stable combination. Even at school, we tend to be good at one and not the other, for instance.

The problem is that students studying jazz guitar are crying out for a system to aid them. A set of dos and don'ts; hard and fast rules which work every time and it's always tough when you have to break the news to all those eager faces that there aren't any such things.

All I can offer is guidance, and the guidance I'm personally most qualified to give is to tell you how I learned to do what I do with a guitar and hope that it will shed some light on your own studies.

I want to steer well away from academic measures to make the jazz magic work, too. There are plenty of books out there that will tell you the musical whys and wherefores for everything you read in this book. I want to try and keep things as simple as I can.

Nobody can expect to take on a task like learning a musical instrument without part of the onus being upon themselves to go and do some research. Asking the right questions and looking in the right areas to find the answers is all part of the game and so I'm going to be setting homework all the way through this tutor!

I thought it would be useful if I could set out the strategy that will gradually unfold as you follow the lessons in this book right at the beginning. More and more I come across manuals for electronic machines like computers or guitar effects which have a 'quick start' section at the beginning, giving the proud new owner the optimum chance of getting somewhere with their new merchandise as soon as possible. I think it's a great idea and intend to try and implement it here. So here is a 'quick start' guide for learning chord melody guitar playing…

Quick Start Chord Melody

1. You are going to need some jazz standards. I'll leave the choice up to you - learn your favorites. I've made some suggestions (see page 11) and given you my reasons for choosing the ones that I have.

In order to learn your set of around 20 standards, you'll need to get your hands on one of the many 'real' or 'fake' books on the market. These are books which contains many hundreds of standards with just the melody line and chord symbols. Even if you're going to mess around with the harmony, you need to know where to start.

2. Learn to look at your fretboard so that you see the lower two strings (the E and A) as your bass strings, your top strings as melody and middle strings as harmony. This is covered more fully in the chapter called 'Fretboard Geography' (page 14).

3. Train your right hand in basic fingerstyle skills. If you're used to playing with a pick, this will take some time, but if you've already made inroads, then the refinements offered in the chapter 'The Right Hand' will help you significantly.

4. Increase your listening time. If you're learning a standard, don't be content with seeking out one player's version of it, find as many as you can. This way, you'll be introduced to the art of arranging

by hearing how different musicians approach a tune. Go and see live jazz, too; there is a lot to be learned here.

I learned an awful lot about arranging almost subconsciously by listening to Nelson Riddle, Frank Sinatra and Nat King Cole. We'll be taking a good look at arranging in the chapter 'The Danny Boy Variations'.

Scales

Although this book is concerned primarily with chord melody playing, the subject of scales is bound to arise and I thought I'd share a few impressions I have concerning them.

If you read the chapter about chords and how I think that guitarists have been slaves to chord charts for far too long, then I'd have to say that I'm of a similar opinion when it comes to scales. An awful lot of faith is placed in learning scales and formulae on how to employ them over various changes and I think that guitarists have been seriously side-tracked on this subject for years. Maybe it's the fact that jazz is dominated by soloists playing strictly melodic instruments. As an instrument in jazz, harmonically the guitar loses out to the piano. And, if that wasn't bad enough, melodically we lose out to the saxophone. But, when the guitar is given the autonomy of harmony and melody combined, it's in a class of its own.

The classical guitar shares the jazz guitar's maverick position in its own particular world. Its quiet voice has been at the mercy of classical composers who have little, or at best limited, knowledge of its workings to the extent that it has a comparatively tiny repertoire.

Small wonder that guitarists in general tend to be loners.

I learned jazz by listening to music and being shown things by a few people. Then I learned many of my hardest and best lessons on the bandstand itself. Most importantly, I learned by playing tunes, not exercises. Scales are all well and good for mapping out the fretboard and for giving you basic technique, but that, in my opinion, is where it ends. I believe there is more virtue to learning melodies, standards or whatever because what you learn will be more directly useful to you. Before the days when we have colleges to study jazz in, an awful lot of knowledge was gained by playing in after hours jam sessions and informal get togethers. Musicians learned how to play over changes by trial and error; they learned the difference between chord tones, scales tones and chromatic tones. They learned how to phrase their solos effectively by listening to each other play.

If I was to give my own impressions, I would say that the only scale you need worry about is the chromatic scale, which is the easiest to remember because it calls for you to play every note on the fretboard between two roots. When a musician learns to play, and equally importantly 'hear', the chromatic scale, he probably has armed himself with the most creative means of expression available to him.

If you want a chart to illustrate what I mean, here goes: say the chord we want to play over is a G7.

Root note	G	1
Chord tones	G B D F	1 3 5 $\flat$7
Scale tones	A C E	2 4 6
Chromatic tones	G$\sharp$ B$\flat$ C$\sharp$ D$\sharp$ F$\sharp$	$\flat$2 $\sharp$2 $\sharp$4 $\sharp$5 maj 7

In effect, we've designated every note in the chromatic scale for use over the chord. In terms of how fail safe the notes would sound, here's another chart:

Root note	G	Very good
Chord tones	G B D F	Great
Scale tones	A C E	Safe
Chromatic tones	G$\sharp$ B$\flat$ C$\sharp$ D$\sharp$ F$\sharp$	Use with caution

Maybe you can see that, rather than learning a whole lot of scale shapes which would accompany a single chord, this is a way to visualize things where, technically speaking, you have everything available to you at any one time.

If there is one problem with the chromatic scale on the guitar fretboard, it's that it doesn't sit under the fingers too conveniently. It takes five frets per string to cater for it - unless you play more diagonally, like this:

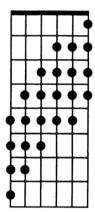

A chromatic scale going 'diagonally' across the fretboard

Or play with a lot of position changes:

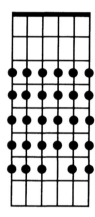

A chromatic scale going across the fretboard using 'five fret' fingering

This may explain why a lot of jazz guitarists seem to have more of a 'horizontal' aspect on the fretboard, moving 'up and down', rather than a rock player, who might view it 'across' from side to side.

If you want a method, I'd say that on any given chord, you're using scale tones to get from chord tone to chord tone and using chromatic tones to get between scale tones.

Play through any chord arrangement merely arpeggiating the chords (and if you can't do this, then you know where your work in this area must begin) and you'll hear how 'safe' everything sounds. But it needs some scale tones in there to offer variety. Simply playing chord tones over the chord is very static, you need something to give the impression of movement. So, next you try adding the scale tones as stepping stones between the chord tones. When you're happy with the result, try adding the odd chromatic tone in between the scale tones.

Players who have learned jazz by associating scales to chords often lack a natural flow in their playing; it sounds too much like jazz by numbers. To me, this approach sounds cold and calculated, whereas chromatic notes, bent notes and the microtones they produce can do an awful lot to warm a solo up. The phrasing starts to sound like it's turning corners and going somewhere. Certainly, thinking about the guitar fingerboard, familiarizing yourself with chromatic tones will do a lot in getting you out of playing in 'box positions'.

Not that I am saying that a jazz player doesn't have to be aware of scales, modes and harmony – quite the reverse – you must know those things. But there are other things which never seem to be taught.

Recommended Standards

A few moments ago I promised you a list of standards which form something of a central core of recommended study material in the jazz guitar chord melody idiom. All these tunes have been recorded often in the past - I've recorded all of them, certainly - and so it will be of enormous value to you to get hold of the music to all of them. By familiarizing yourself with the melody and harmony of these pieces, you will be taking a huge first step towards working on arrangement ideas of your own.

I Got Rhythm	(Gershwin)
I Thought About You	(Van Heusen)
Emily	(Mandell)
All The Things You Are	(Kern)
Stella By Starlight	(Young - Washington)
Taking A Chance On Love	(Duke - Fetter - Latouche)
Willow Weep For Me	(Ronell)
Nuages	(Reinhardt - Larue)
Here's That Rainy Day	(Van Heusen)
I Can't Give You Anything But Love	(Fields - McHugh)
My Funny Valentine	(Rodgers - Hart)
I Remember Clifford	(Golson)
They Can't Take That Away From Me	(Gershwin)
I Get Along Without You Very Well	(Carmichael)
Stardust	(Carmichael)
It Had To Be You	(Kahn - Jones)
Autumn Leaves	(Kosma)
Misty	(Garner)
Honeysuckle Rose	(Waller - Razaf)
Night And Day	(Porter)

Which Key?

Choosing an appropriate key for a piece can be a crucial element in making it work. The great composers chose to flex their compositional muscles in various keys to good effect, claiming that each brought a different characteristic to a piece.

Let's dispose of a few myths...
It's a complete myth that all jazz tunes have to be played in 'flat' key signatures like B♭ or A♭. This was mainly a courtesy paid to horn players for whom those keys meant an easy fingering on their instruments - never mind about the guitar player, he'll just have to fit in! Well, when we're playing unaccompanied, we call the shots and so I tend to play in more guitar friendly key signatures than perhaps you would expect.
The majority of jazz musicians play these tunes in their 'written keys' which tend to be in flat key signatures for B♭ and E♭ instruments like horns or saxes.
There are many jazz musicians who believe that the written key in the only key and will not play in any other.

The student should learn a tune in its written key and then experiment by transposing it to other keys, as different keys will bring out different colors, sounds and moods to the tune.

To my mind, flat keys tend to sound darker and sharp keys are more open and bright sounding. Learn each standard in every key. It will help inspire you and search for new ideas. I'm of the opinion that you should find the key that sounds and feels right for you and your instrument.

Don't be put off by thinking that some keys will mean that you cannot use any open strings. Playing a low open E in B♭ gives you your flattened fifth for example, and can be very effective.

List of guitarists to check out

There really is nothing more valuable than listening to the acknowledged masters of chord melody playing for inspiration and ideas. If you're working on a particular song from the jazz repertoire, you can bet that it's been recorded many times in the past and seeking out a few alternate versions will broaden your own outlook considerably. Of course, it doesn't need to be a solo guitar rendition; remember that I took a lot of my arrangement ideas from big band recordings. But a look over the fence into someone else's chord melody back yard occasionally will inspire you and temper everything you've learned.

I've included a list of players below whom I would thoroughly recommend you to seek out. It's not exhaustive, and please accept my blushing apologies if I've missed anyone out!

Ike Isaacs
Chet Atkins
Joe Pass
Barney Kessel
Tuck Andress
Charlie Byrd
Ted Greene
George Van Eps
Lenny Breau

TUNING

It's amazing how often this fundamental element of playing the guitar can be underestimated. A quick consultation with an electronic tuner and the job's finished; but there's more to the task of tuning than that. In these days of equal temperament, tuning the guitar is, at best, a compromise between pure science and what the ear determines as being 'right'. I tune the guitar in the same way a piano is tuned, in fifths, and believe that this is one way that the instrument can be brought in tune with itself.

Why the guitar can never be exactly 'in tune'
The guitar is a fickle instrument, when it comes to tuning. Science can prove quite adequately that the instrument is set up to get the best average results over the length of the fretboard and, in fact, can never be exact, no matter what means are used to try and bring this about.
You'll be aware how important it is to get the notes at the 12th fret of the guitar in tune with the open strings. By adjusting the bridge so that everything tallies at this point, it means that your tuning is tolerable for the first 12 frets in any case. But even a guitar which has been tuned using the most accurate digital tuner you can find is still not going to be in tune with itself at every point on the fretboard. So tuning is maybe not the exact science you thought it was when you tuned your guitar with a little box of tricks you thought was solving all your problems.

I actually tune my guitar to A = 442, whereas the standard is A = 440. I do this because I'm playing clean and using no vibrato and I find it makes the guitar sound 'right' to me. It means that my guitar is very slightly sharp, according to the rest of the world. When I say 'slightly' sharp, I mean it. Many tuners have the facility to alter their tuning calibration and, if you own one of these, try recalibrating it to 442 and tune your guitar to it. You may notice a difference, but it's hardly perceptible. Interestingly, this idea of tuning slightly sharp is by no means new. The lead horns in big band brass sections have been using this trick for years in order to help their instruments 'stand out' from the rank and file.
As an aside, it's interesting how our perception of pitch has changed over the last few hundred years. Since the 16th Century, our conception of pitch in general has risen by two to three semitones, so back then, the value of A would have been around 415.
Anyway, back to tuning with fifths. A fifth is the most musically accurate interval to tune with. Piano tuners have been using this method for years and it's no coincidence. You might be tempted to think that the third is the most consonant interval in music, but it's no good for tuning. The reason for this is that the harmonics of the major third start going out of tune when you reach their high harmonics, whereas a fifth remains pure right up to inaudible harmonic levels. If you're curious about how this works, look up 'the overtone series' in a science book and all will be revealed.
My ideas on tuning are very personal and are something I have developed over the years.
Firstly, my bridge is set slightly sharp so that, past the twelfth fret, the notes become very slightly sharper. This is a way of compensating for the fact that the top strings in particular become flat the more you play, due to small build-ups of sweat from the fingers.
It's a fact that, if you tune slightly sharp, only a few people will notice it, but if you tune flat, everybody, including their dog, will hear it and feel uncomfortable, even if they don't know why!
I tune my top E string very slightly sharp for the same reason, but the bass E is tuned very slightly flat because the harder you strike the bottom string, the more it will vibrate, causing it to go sharp naturally.
I also tune my third string (G) slightly flat as it always sounds sharp to me when tuned using an electronic tuner. This problem is even more noticeable when using a plain third on a nylon string guitar.

Fretboard Geography

I thought that a few words regarding simple orientation on your instrument might be called for. One of the most important elements to mastering the guitar is to be well versed in fretboard geography. But the guitar is a fickle master and its diversity is such that many different 'maps' of the same terrain are available.

An important part of removing the fear of the unknown as far as chord voicings are concerned is to learn a system of chord recognition, which involves a lot less work than some would think. We look at the CAGED system in the chapter on chords. This kind of fretboard 'orienteering' should make up at least some small part of your every day practice routine; start off testing yourself by finding three different barre chord shapes for the major, minor or seventh chords and gradually increase the difficulty of the task. You'll soon find that the guitar neck doesn't look such a scary place.

It's important, too, to have a working idea of where all the notes are on the neck. There are players who will come to the instrument so totally instinctively that the actual naming of notes - or any naming convention, for that matter - is immaterial. Their innate sense of musicianship will lead the way and putting a name to anything they do is secondary. But, in the main, any device which helps you learn or communicate with other guitarists/musicians is going to be of great help.

Use every trick available to you; write out a chart showing where all the notes are on the guitar fretboard and keep it somewhere in sight when you practice. Continually test yourself and gradually the fretboard will cease to be that uncharted terrain it so often tends to be!

DON'T CALL THEM CHORDS

There is a popular image of a jazz guitarist as being a walking encyclopedia of the most awkward and contrived chords imaginable. Another myth centers around the idea that a jazz musician uses chords that are somehow secret or shady and definitely never shown in any respectable, commercially available chord book... So I thought I'd take the opportunity to put the record straight. When I sat down to think about the contents of this book, I wondered if I'd be able to get through it without mentioning the word 'chord' at all. For years jazz guitarists have been hidebound by chord arrangements and chord shapes. It's a hangover from the big band days where the guitar's function was that of pure rhythm and very little else. For solo guitar arrangements, the concept of merely superimposing melody over block chords is not exploiting the full potential of the instrument. My own perspective on arrangement brings the guitar more in line with its classical cousin, where music is arranged contrapuntally. Nobody who is at all aware of classical guitar playing would expect to be handed a chord chart for a piece by Bach - and so why apply that kind of thinking to the music of Gershwin, Cole Porter and Van Heusen?

I believe that the 'old school' thinking can hold back the progress of the would-be chord/melody guitarist. Once the 'shackles' have been thrown off, one is left with the pure basics of melody, harmony and rhythm and allows more interesting and creative ideas to the fore.

Guitar chord box drudgery

I think that things would be better if students were taught to abandon the concept of chord 'shapes' per se and learn to look at a tune from the separate, but entirely compatible, elements of melody, rhythm and harmony.

I learned an awful lot about harmony by listening to band arrangements early on. I'd hear that the band wasn't just playing a straightforward chordal accompaniment to the melody, but the various instruments were playing counter melodies which moved around and against the main theme. When I started to work out my own arrangements for guitar I tried to think how various tunes might be arranged in a similar way. This is why you'll rarely hear me playing a melody with a series of static chords underneath. Usually, I try to think of combining different moving lines together to make the thing breathe a little more.

Of course, I did spend years on the bandstand playing chordal accompaniment for soloists - and I did exactly that for Stephane Grappelli, too. So I put my time in learning chord 'shapes'.

If I was going to recommend a system whereby a student could learn the 'essentials' as far as chords are concerned, then it would be to learn as many tunes as you can. If you're learning from a 'real' book, you'll certainly come across chords that are new to you at first and will probably have to look them up or work them out. But, as you progress, you'll find that you need to do this less and less. Then, when it comes time to start working on your own chord melody arrangement, the simple fact that you will trying to put the melody on the top strings will force you to find different voicings for all the chords you've learned.

I would also recommend the virtues of 'less is more' as far as voicing are concerned. You very rarely find a jazz guitarist playing six string chords under a soloist - that's another hang over from the big band era. If your function is to provide an interesting harmonic backdrop for a soloist, then you want to escape the four to the bar, six string rhythm regime as soon as possible.

What chords are and why we shouldn't be afraid not to use them

Time for a little straightforward theory - don't worry, it's really quite simple and might help you understand a little bit about dissonance and consonance in music.

Jazz chords are famous for containing everything including the kitchen sink. With titles like E♭13♭9, it's no wonder that students of jazz tend to feel a little lost. Jazz guitar students in particular can find themselves completely floored because the guitar is not laid out in such a 'linear' way as the piano.

Pianists get that little bit of extra help with theory because they have more obvious signposts; a piano has a single key for middle C - we have five positions where you can find that particular pitch. And so on. Come to that, most harmony books out there are written in such a way that they can be understood pretty much only from the point of view of a keyboard - so where does that leave us?

In order to throw a little light where it's needed, let's start off by looking at the basic building blocks of harmony - intervals. As you probably know, chords are notes sounded together to produce harmony and it's not just a random choice, either. There are rules that are usually obeyed - a major chord contains the first, third and fifth members of its relative scale - and so on. But the trouble usually starts when harmony becomes more complicated than that.

We're going to look at those building blocks of harmony - and we'll start with the intervals of the scales themselves.

The most important place to start is to play the intervals against a static root note and hear what they all sound like. You should be able to hear how some of them are sweet and pleasant sounding, while others are harsh and don't sound nice at all.

Do this exercise in the key of C Major: play the notes C and D, the first two notes of the C scale, together. What do they sound like to you? Bitter or sweet?

Next, play C and E. How do you think they sound together? Then, play the remaining notes of the scale with C and make a note of how each interval sounds to you.

If your answers tally with the majority vote, you'll probably have decided that C and E, C and G and C and A sounded nice, whereas C and D, C and F and C and B enjoyed varying degrees of nastiness.

Out of all of the intervals, you might decide that C and E sounded sweetest and C and B sounded not well at all. Out of interest, some people find C and F quite reasonable while others think it's awful - it's a split vote.

So it's easy to understand that nice happy major chords contain notes from the first group - C Major is made up with the notes C, E and G. But it would be wrong to assume that any chord from the ugly bunch is going to sound bad. Play a Cmaj7 chord: sounds OK, doesn't it? But if you study the chord, you'll see that it contains both C and B - the worst sounding interval of the bunch. And yet, the resulting chord is amongst the sweetest around and yet you've proved to yourself that it contains a 'nasty' interval. How does this work? Where does the dissonance disappear to, exactly?

The answer to this is also the answer to a much bigger question - that of how dissonance is used in music as a whole. It's a question of balance; in the chord of Cmaj7, you've got present the very strong and sweet relationship of both C and E plus C and G. In adding the dissonance of C to B, instead of creating a bad sounding chord, the dissonance is offset and smoothed out. But it's still there.

This goes for a lot of jazz harmony - it's a balancing act. There are chords that sound tense and full of dissonance (usually because they contain more than a single dissonant interval so the balance is thrown over to 'bitter' rather than 'sweet') and they create tension in the music - but they are usually always 'resolved' pretty quickly by something 'sweet'.

Remember, I'm not going to talk rocket science here, just cover the ground and try to demystify things a little for you.

If all the various scale tones from C major are put in a chord form, we end up with a family of major chords which all have a different character and are consequently useful in different chord melody situations as alternatives for a simple major chord.

First of all, here's a scale of C major:

C D E F G A B C
1 2 3 4 5 6 7 8

It's really just the musical alphabet from C to C with straightforward numbers underneath. So, if I asked you what the root, third and fifth of C major are, you could check and see that they are C, E and G. So, if I told you that a C6 chord was just the root, third, fifth and sixth notes of the C major scale, it wouldn't take you long to come to the conclusion that we're talking about a C major chord with an A in it somewhere.

If you check, you'll find that, in both cases, the note which has been superimposed on the familiar C maj chord shapes is an A.

Now take a look at this:

C	D	E	F	G	A	B	C	D	E	F	G	A	B	C
1	2	3	4	5	6	7	8	9	3	11	5	13	7	1

Please feel free to go and have a quick lie down if the above scale seems a little confusing at first, it won't in a minute.

What we have here is merely two octaves of C major, written out with numbers underneath again - but written out the way that music convention dictates (so, for once, it's not jazz's fault that it looks confusing.). This kind of thinking was about long before jazz was invented and all that's happened is that, when we continue above the octave, instead of using numbers in strict sequential order, we keep those important numbers from before - that is to say we keep the 1, 3, 5 and 7 - and use 9, 11 and 13 for the notes D, F and A respectively.

If this sounds daft to you, remember that we're dealing with some of the rules of music theory that have existed since before the time of Bach. And if you think of some of the other ideas that were around then… We might have put a man on the moon, but in many ways music still prefers to travel by horse and cart.

If you're unsure about a note's dual identity, subtract seven from it and you'll end up with its original position in the scale. That is, if you've forgotten what a 13th is, take seven away and it returns to its former self, a 6th. I know it's confusing at first, but stick with it.

So this now opens up the whole of the major chord family - it's easy to see which notes have been superimposed on the triad. Here are a few examples:

A Cmaj9 is root, third, fifth, seventh and ninth. Check the scale above and you'll see that this is merely a C, E, G, B and D.

A C6/9 (sometimes called a 'six add nine') is a root, third, fifth, sixth and ninth.

A Cadd9 is root, third, fifth and ninth.

It's almost like basic shorthand - there's nothing arcane, secret or particularly magic here. Chord symbols are usually straightforward abbreviations of what notes they contain.

Up pops the Devil…
A few hundred years ago, the church, which was the biggest employer of composers, banned the use of the interval known as the flat fifth. They referred to it as 'The Devil's Interval' - or 'diabolus in musica' if you prefer the original Latin - and there was a lot of superstition surrounding it.

The reason for their fear was because the flat fifth lies exactly in the middle of the chromatic scale - it inverts to itself, which means that it's always the same distance from the root from above or below.

C C♯ D E♭ E F F♯ G G♯ A B♭ B C

In the case of the chromatic scale above, F♯ is the diabolical element. Count either up or down from one of the C notes and you'll find that F♯ is dead centre. This, of course, isn't true of any other interval and what's more, the flat fifth doesn't sound particularly nice, either. Obviously the work of the horned one!

It was probably JS Bach who finally exorcised the flat fifth and returned it to good use in religious music. The flat fifth is a natural resident in a diminished chord and crops up in dominant sevenths, too, and so you can see how hard it was to resist the interval's diabolical charm.

This uncomfortable sounding interval would have certainly jarred our ancestors' nerves, but it is the same 'uncomfortableness' which gives a lot of contemporary music its edge. The flat fifth is used a lot in jazz and blues harmony and, as a consequence both are often referred to as 'The Devil's Music'.

Homework

If you own a chord book, look up the major chord symbols and try to work out exactly which notes of the scale have been added to make up the chord. Then, listen to them all and try to decide for yourself how they sound - it's a little like trying to say how wine tastes. You can use words like complex, bland, sweet and so on, but it's important to catalogue them all using your own criteria. That way, you'll know how they fit in with your ideas when you come to start making your own arrangements of tunes.

Myth busting

If I had to answer a few frequently asked questions regarding chords and their place in jazz guitar, it might go something like this:

1) You don't need to play a different chord on every beat
2) You don't need to harmonize a melody with a different chord for every note
3) Your choice of chord doesn't have to be heavily weighted with dissonance - don't use a 13♭9♯5 when a straightforward major will do

Also, jazz students can very quickly become obsessed with chord substitution - more jazz mathematics. When we talked about scales and found that there really is only one worth worrying about - the chromatic scale - there is a very similar thing to consider when we come around to talking about chord substitution. Listen to this, it will save you an awful lot of grief...

Generally speaking, any melody note can be supported by any chord. The only thing to be aware of is that some will sound better than others and the chances are that only a couple will sound dead right.

The natural way to learn about what chord fits where is, once again, to learn arrangements of as many tunes as you can. You will get many of the pointers you need from doing this and if you keep your ears wide open while you do it, you'll find that you can call on a lot of the information you're taking in later on.

I'm aware of a lot of the theory behind chord voicings and so on, but I never let it affect my choice - which is instinctive and generally spontaneous. If you free yourself from the confines of jazz science and tell yourself that you're going to make your own rules, you're going to be far closer to defining a style of your own.

One of the reasons why I wanted to try and not mention the word 'chord' in this book at all is that, for me, the melody is all-important - and I hardly play chords at all during a chord melody piece. Listen carefully to any of my recordings; I rarely use any 'block chords' at all, it's all moving lines and any actual harmony occurs only where those lines converge. In fact, most of the time, I'm rarely playing more than two notes at the same time.

If you look at the chapter on 'tenths', you'll get a good idea of how I go about putting together one of these arrangements. Every tune has an essential outline or shape. That shape is derived principally from the tune's melody (the strongest part) supported by the bass and filled out by its harmony. If you want to understand a tune, your most important task is to learn its melody. Then, using the system we evolve in our look at tenths, support the melody by introducing a bass part. Nothing fancy at first, a simple root will do nicely. By all means observe the chords, but don't let them dominate your sense of arrangement; dip into the harmony, but use it sparingly and colorfully. Remember that often two notes will say more than six. Think of the tune's rhythm, its feel and try to explore ideas of your own.

In fact, that's another mistake many jazz players make when they're new to this kind of playing - they don't state the original melody clearly enough and everything becomes unclear and messy. Really, the melody is the most important part - don't bury it.

Personally, I tend to think of chords in terms of color; different chords produce different effects and textures on a song's harmonic 'landscape' and the choice of which one to use is a far more natural process than is often assumed. I can give you the colors and shapes I see, if you like, but it all becomes a little esoteric and probably of no use to the student.

We've only really scratched the surface of building chord textures – but all the way along the line, the principle remains almost exactly the same. Minor chords are built from a minor triad, based on a minor scale, sevenths are build upon a basic four note framework (1 3 5 ♭7), but each time, you are merely adding notes from the scale, changing the color of the chord.

When a jazz player meets a tune he wants to play, he will look for its basic chord structure by reducing all the chords it contains to basic majors, minors, sevenths and so on. This will represent the song in its most basic form and it is then ready to be rebuilt from his own pre-programmed palette of chord textures. Part of the process of re-building comes from the player's experience – a considerable dalliance with chords and voicings, which will have been constantly sorted and sifted quite naturally during the process of learning about jazz. But the work starts with a few simple experiments like the ones I've shown you here.

Chord systems

There are a few systems for understanding chords on the fretboard, which aim to free the guitarist from the routine of constantly checking a chord book to find a particular voicing for a chord. One of the better known is called the 'CAGED' system and, very briefly, it goes something like this:
If we consider the chord of C major, you'll probably be aware of its basic position on the fretboard - the one we discover pretty early on in the learning process:

C major

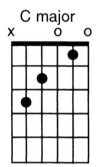

As you progress with your learning, you find that C is available elsewhere on the neck; the same notes, but in a different location. We find it as a barre chord on the third fret, for instance:

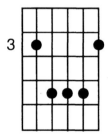

This chord shape resembles a basic A shape and is known as the 'A shape barre chord for C' by people who tend toward long-winded names for chord shapes.

Moving up the fretboard, C checks in again in the fifth position:

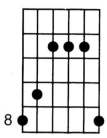

This shape looks like a G shape down at the nut. The next one looks familiar, too:

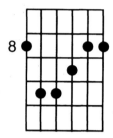

This C chord at the eighth fret looks very much like an open E. Finally, we get this shape at the tenth fret:

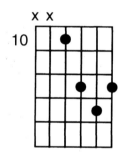

Now we've covered the entire fretboard with different versions of a basic C chord and the shapes of the chords spell out C A G E D.

This is an important first step in learning to visualize the fretboard, because the trick works in every key. Try it in E and you'll find that your first shape down at the nut is, obviously, an 'E shape' for E major. So the shape you're looking for next is D (2nd position) then the C, A and G shapes fall into line up the fretboard.

One of the principal advantages with this system is that it means that if you know a handful of voicings based on a C shape - C6, Cmaj7, C9 and so on, you can very quickly apply them to other keys. It multiplies your knowledge of chords by twelve at a stroke (twelve keys per chord shape). So, by learning some of the more basic chord shapes available to you, you've actually got hundreds under your hands at any one time. Then, if you're looking for a particular chord at a particular point on the fretboard, you only need think about the nearest shape from the CAGED system.

This system takes a while to learn, but it's been recommended by jazz players for generations as a way of systemizing your learning.

Turnarounds

A few of you might be wanting a definition of the word 'turnaround' in its musical sense - and so, here goes. A turnaround is the final few bars in a chord arrangement before it returns to the top of the tune. In a twelve bar blues, for example, it will be the last couple of bars, when the chords feel like they're 'turning around' to start all over again.

In a jazz context the turnaround measures (or bars) in a song are often quite 'busy' harmonically speaking and players often choose to fill them with some phrases which punctuate the main melody and gently draw things back around to the top of the tune. I've recorded some examples of what you can do with a very common turnaround chord arrangement. The basic chords I'm playing over are these:

|| Emin7 / A7/ | Dmin / G7 / | Cmaj / / / ||

Don't Call Them Chords

Don't become unnecessarily concerned with what I'm playing - although, obviously, study the music and tab - the most important thing here is that you listen to the effect these turnarounds have and how they relate firstly to the chord series above, and secondly how they relate to each other. Don't just learn to play them, try to understand them, too!

Incidentally, if these first examples don't make too much sense to you structurally - that is, you can't quite see where the chord forms are coming from, don't worry, we're covering this ground in the next chapter. I just thought I'd offer a few examples on turnarounds while we were on the subject.

More on chords...

While we're here, I'll add a word or two more about chords. You may have noticed that a series of 7th chords sound restless and unresolved and, as such, probably wouldn't do as the chord structure under a ballad or song in their own right. There are technical reasons for this (I'll try to be gentle) namely that they belong to the cycle of fourths - which isn't an exclusive club for bicycling enthusiasts, but a harmonic phenomenon which permeates every area of music. The cycle of fourths is merely the way in which dominant seventh chords resolve into each other. They don't relate to any one specific key.

You'll have noticed that, if you're in the key of C, then the chord of G7 is nearly always used as a means to bring the chord arrangement 'home' to C. Play this example:

$$ \| \text{C} / / / \mid \text{F} / / / \mid \text{G7} / / / \mid \text{C} / / / \| $$

Can you hear how the G7 leads your ear comfortably back to C again? This is the main job of a dominant seventh chord; it sets up a resolution. But dominant chords also resolve into each other - that's to say that G7 resolves into C, but it will also fit snugly into C7, too. And C7 has a sort of fatal attraction to F (you'll notice that these chords are all a fourth apart).

So this chord arrangement sounds perfectly OK, although it's anything but diatonic:

$$ \| \text{C7} / / / \mid \text{F7} / / / \mid \text{B}\flat\text{7} / / / \mid \text{E}\flat\text{7} / / / \| $$

The only problem with it is it doesn't actually sound like it's coming to a conclusion at any point. Jazz musicians and classical composers both use the cycle of fourths as a sort of compass to navigate between keys or suspend resolution and that's why the last example sounds a little 'unfinished' or 'unresolved'. In context it will work fine, but it wouldn't necessarily suit as the basis to a melody.

TENTHS

In this chapter, I hope to be able to answer the question, 'Exactly where do you start when you're putting together a solo chord melody piece for guitar?' It's not an easy question to answer, because there's not just the one way of going about things. But if people are looking to understand the fundamentals of putting a solo piece together, then there are a few things which will help you on your path.

We're going to be looking at the very core of putting a chord melody arrangement together. We'll consider setting up a framework which will establish a solid foundation on which to build.

For now, the two most important things you need to know are the whys and wherefores of an interval known as a tenth and how to base a chord on every note of the scale.

Tenths

If you've read through the previous chapter you'll hopefully have quite a clear picture of intervals and their place in music and harmony. We've seen that an interval is the way of measuring the distance between notes in musical terms. We've already met thirds, fourths and so on and have seen that the distance along the scale between C and E is called a third because it covers three notes inclusively:

C D E
1 2 3

The distance between C and G is known as a fifth for similar reasons:

C D E F G
1 2 3 4 5

We're not going to go into a great amount of detail on this point and I would recommend that, if this process is still a little mysterious, you seek out one of the commonly available theory books which will provide you with all the detail you need.

The interval we want to concern ourselves with here is known as a 'tenth' which is a third with an octave's gap in the middle:

C D E F G A B C D E
1 2 3 4 5 6 7 8 9 10

It's still C to E, but it covers a bit more of an area on the fretboard. Again, not wanting to go into too much detail about intervals, there is such a thing as a minor tenth, but the principal remains the same – look at the C minor scale:

C D E♭ F G A♭ B♭ C D E♭
1 2 3 4 5 6 7 8 9 10

The same numbering system applies, only the key signature has changed.

As you'll soon see, there's a lot to be done with major and minor tenths.

The Harmonized Scale

If we take a major scale, we can build a chord on every note by stacking up notes a third apart. When we look at a scale which has been harmonized using stacked thirds, we get this effect:

Fifths:	G A B C D E F G
Thirds (aka tenths):	E F G A B C D E
Roots:	C D E F G A B C

You see how the scale has been 'folded over' upon itself so that you could say it merely starts from three different points – C for the bottom line, E for the middle line and G for the top. Everything remains parallel and completely symmetrical.
Naturally, these chords have names:

Cmaj Dmin Emin Fmaj Gmaj Amin Bdiminished Cmaj

Something they all have in common is a third – major for the major chords and minor for the minors – and so, naturally, they have a tenth each, too. Here's what tenths look like on the fretboard:

Exs 4.1 & 4.2

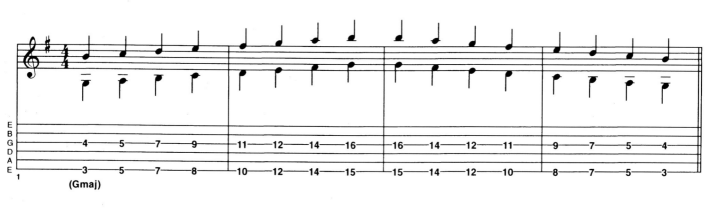

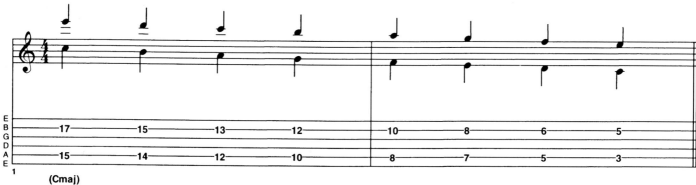

On the CD, I've played a series of tenths firstly in G, with the bass notes on the sixth string and the tenths on the third, then in C, with the bass on the fifth string and the tenths on the second.
If you play through the examples above, you should be able to hear how the scale has been harmonized each time. Now, every note has a basic harmonic partner, forming a sort of skeletal system for the whole scale. Remember, melodies come from scales and so you should be able to see that, even with a device as basic and as simple as this one, we've got a series of powerful tools at our disposal.
Next, we'll fill in the gaps between some of the notes to make everything flow a little better. Even though these gaps are filled by non-scale tones, they sound perfectly in place. In fact, they help the ear. Essentially what's happened is we've filled in some of the gaps in order to make things flow a little better.

Ex 4.3

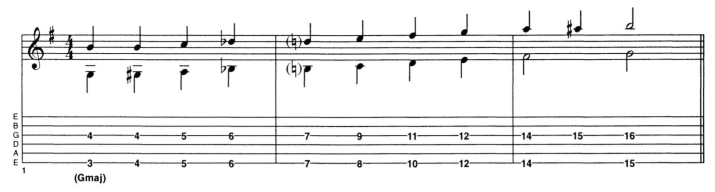

Now, to fill things out even further, we're going to add a seventh to each chord.

Ex 4.4

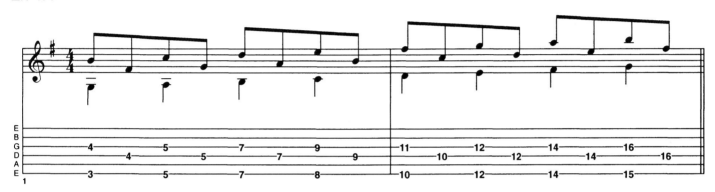

Finally in this section, we're going to introduce some movement around the seventh.

Ex 4.5

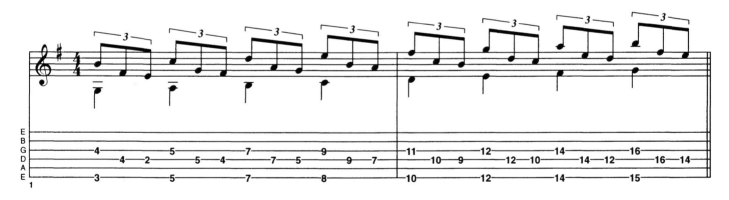

So now, we have a root, third (tenth) and seventh built on each scale tone and you should be able to hear how full everything is already beginning to sound – and we're not finished yet. Essentially, what's happening here is that we have a bass note with a 'chord' on top - that's two parts out of three. Put a melody on top and you've got the fundamentals right in front of you.

Listen to the CD, play the examples yourself and remember what everything looks like on the guitar fingerboard. Most importantly, try to remember the sound that these intervals make when played together.

Review

You'll probably have been surprised to hear just how full sounding this relationship between a root and its third can be. In many ways, the root and third are the two most important notes in any cord; together they are capable of signposting either a major or minor chord sound – and that's sometimes all you need to put across an awful lot of harmonic information.

In order to do some practical work on the subject of tenths, I want you to play a G major scale on your bass E string:

G A B C D E F♯ G
1 2 3 4 5 6 7 1

When you've done that, add the tenth interval on the G string. There are only two types to worry about, major or minor. Your first tenth will contain G (third fret, bass E string) and B (fourth fret, G string). Remember the shape – there's only one other to learn. The second tenth will have A on the bass (fifth fret, bass E string) and C (fifth fret, G string). As a reminder, here's what you're going to play in the form of a chord chart.

Harmonized Scale Of G Major In Tenths:

Gmaj Amin Bmin Cmaj Dmaj E min F♯min
1   2   3   4   5   6   7

Remember, you're using only two shapes on the neck to play this exercise.
When your fingers are familiar with finding the two shapes in their correct places, change the key to A and work it out again. The shapes stay in the same order, you've just to get used to seeing them slightly higher on the neck. Just leave it at root and third for now, worry about filling things out by adding sevenths and so on later.

If you've taken some time to experiment with moving the tenths around the neck, you might have even found that you can play some tunes just by finding the melodies and adding the tenths in around them. The chances are that everything sounded fine, but music relies on something more than just moving blocks of harmony about and, despite the fact that there was a lot of actual physical movement going on, everything still sounds a little 'static'.
So the next step is to begin to add the melody. At the moment, we've established a bass and harmony part, and so melody is the only missing ingredient.

Adding melody using the blues
We'll use the universal language of the blues to help illustrate the point we've reached. This is a blues in G which uses the devices we've been looking at already, but adds a simple little melody on top.
Listen to the CD example to see how full things are sounding – and yet, when you look at the music, you'll see that very little appears to be happening at all.

Ex 4.6

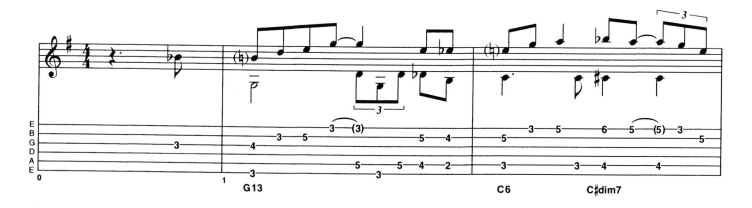

These devices we're looking at are great for making a little seem a lot on the fretboard. But in the next example we're going to see how we can take quite a lot of harmonic information away – literally remove some of the harmonic scaffolding – and still be left with something which sounds full and interesting. In this version of our G blues, the melody becomes the dominating feature and the harmony slips into the background to provide an essential balance.

Ex 4.7

28

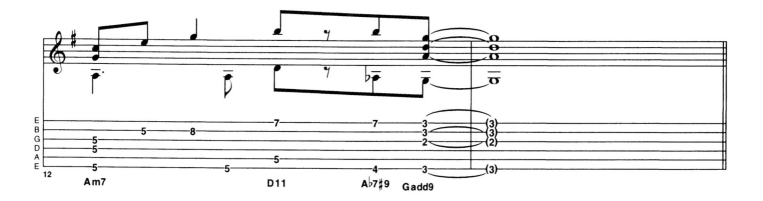

Now don't panic - all we're doing is missing out a bass note here, a chord tone there — and yet the result sounds whole and complete. A lot of guitar solo chord melody work is a conjuring trick where the arrangement sounds very full and rich, and yet there's actually very little going on at all.
We've taken some very positive steps forward from our basic tenths framework. Take every step slowly, remember to play through the examples and listen to the effect produced.

Basslines

First of all, a word or two about bass lines in general. At a guitar seminar once, a student asked the late Joe Pass exactly how to go about adding a walking bass to a melody. Joe's reply was, 'Well, first you've got to know what a bass part sounds like and see if you can play it.' It might sound a very simple and obvious answer, but it's absolutely true; if you don't know what a jazz bass part sounds like in the first place you haven't got a chance of being able to play one which serves the dual roles of supporting the melody and sounding authentic.

In most instances, the bass lines I play tend to sit on the sixth and fifth strings, which means that there is a fair amount of movement along the length of the fretboard. This implies that you've got to become accurate at targeting fretboard positions and a lot of students find that they're initially either overshooting or stopping short. Don't worry, this sort of thing comes with practice, you'll get it in the end, it just seems daunting to begin with.

Another thing about bass parts is that it's unwise to underestimate their importance, musically speaking. If we sneak a look at the pages of classical harmony, we'll see that the bass part is considered only secondary to the melody in importance. This means that even chords are considered subsidiary to melody and bass lines and it might be difficult to understand exactly why this is. To get the message loud and clear, we can look over classical guitar's fence and see what goes on in some pieces there. If you've had any experience playing classical guitar, you'll know that it's quite common for only two notes to be playing at any time and yet the resulting piece sounds full and complete. If you listen to a piece like Bach's E Minor Bouree, I'm sure that you'd agree that it sounds very full indeed, and yet there are very rarely more than two notes being fretted simultaneously. Why is this? Well, for a start, Bach just knew his job. The two parts interweave so effectively that the listener feels that he is listening to something whole and complete - and that's exactly what we aim for when we put a bass line in a solo guitar piece.

Starting out

A good place to start is to look at the changes to a standard. We know that the most important note in a chord is its root and so, just glancing at the chord arrangement, you've got a very powerful place to start assembling your bass line. It's not foolproof, but what system really is? One thing for sure, it's a good way to learn how everything works and so let's take a closer look.

Your standard might have changes that look like this:

| Gmaj / Emin / | Amin / D7 / | Bmin / Emin / | Amin / D7 / | Gmaj /// ||

To begin with, forget the actual chords themselves and take a look at the root notes and their position on the two bass strings. Remember, we're going to add melody and chords on top eventually and so we have to limit the bass to these strings and look at the fretboard more from a 'left to right' perspective.

So, faced with the idea of finding a suitable location for G, E, A, B and D on the fifth and sixth strings, I might decide to play them with the G at the third fret on the bass E, the B at the seventh fret on the sixth string, the E at the seventh fret on the A string, the A on the fifth fret on the E and the D at the fifth on the A string. It's a little bit like 'joining the dots' in children's puzzle books. Actually, that's not a bad way to view it; string the bass notes together in the right way and you do build up the perfect picture of a bass part.

The first thing we'll do is play tenths based on the chord arrangement:

Ex 5.1

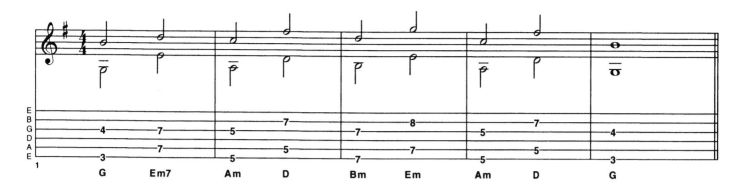

This is now beginning to build our framework. Pay special attention to the bass and make sure that you have something under your fingers that feels comfortable - you don't have to use my fingering, we're all different, find something that works for you.

You'll probably agree that everything sounds fine, but it doesn't exactly sound like a bass part, does it? We need to introduce some movement in order to give it that 'walking bass' feel that jazz bass players try to introduce into everything they play. Having movement in the bass helps everything 'swing' and provides some counterpoint for the melody, so it's important to learn exactly where this movement comes from.

I try not to rely on giving people rules to follow, because it's more often the people who break all the rules who turn out to be the true innovators. So let's just say that there are a few guidelines for constructing a bassline which would be good to take on board.

If you look back at our chord arrangement excerpt you'll see that there are two beats per chord which would imply that you're expected to play each of the bass notes twice. In actual fact, that's what is making everything sound so sluggish. It pins everything down to such an extent that there is hardly any flow at all. So, rule one: you can approach any bass note from either one fret above or below the root.

Sounds a little scary, perhaps, but let's look at what could happen with our chords here.

Ex 5.2

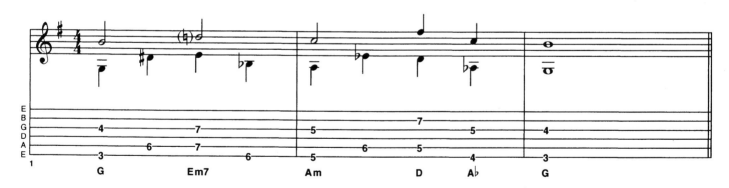

Notice that I'm not repeating the 'melody' note over the chromatic tones. This allows the bass part to have a life of its own and gives the arrangement the beginnings of what could become a punchy rhythm part.

It sounds fine and so let's intensify that bass rhythm a little and see where it leads us:

Ex 5.3

Let's see what happens if we play fuller chords along with the bass part, as opposed to the tenths that we have been using:

Ex 5.4

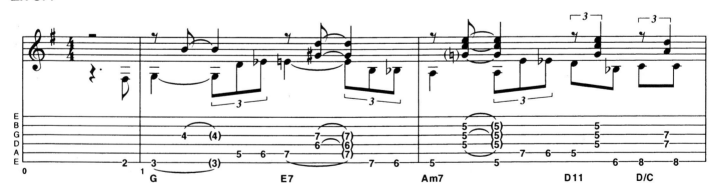

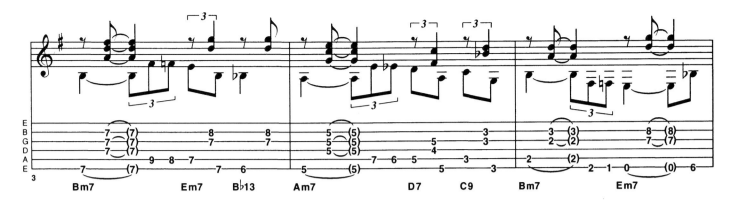

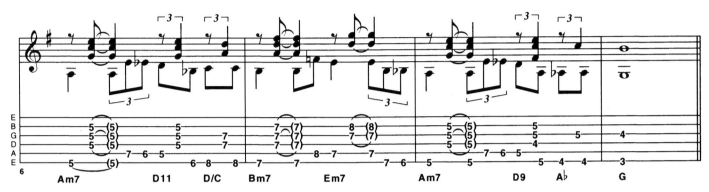

Play the bassline with your thumb and try to get things to swing. Listen to a few bass players and try to imitate their feel.

The sequence I gave you in that last example is a common one in jazz and you'll find it cropping up in many standards (in various keys, of course). If you experiment with it, you'll find other ways of moving the bassline between the chords. Think of it as if you're linking things together, a bit like 'join the dots'!

Rhythm

Just to make sure the idea really comes across, let's look at another style of bass part and find a way of dealing with it. This time, we'll start with a solo bass part and build on it using a couple of rhythmic variations.

Ex 5.5

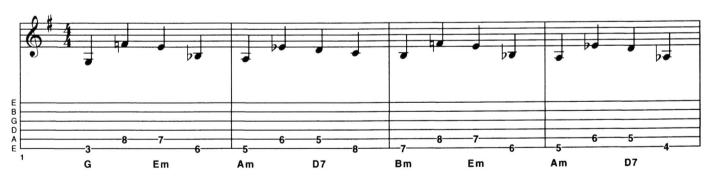

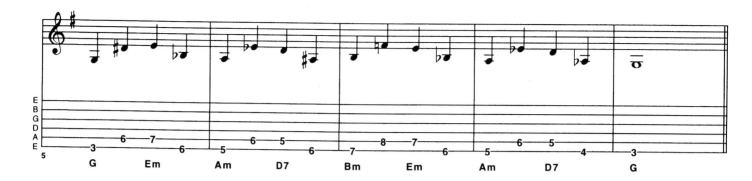

Remember that it's vital to think of your two bottom strings as being the 'bass area' of your guitar. You could play the notes above using the whole breadth of the guitar's fingerboard, but we must leave room for both melody and harmony parts on top. It may take you a while to feel comfortable with all the various position changes. But stay with it; slow things right down if necessary, and you'll soon find that a natural 'flow' starts to take place.

The next thing we'll take a look at is putting some 'offbeats' into our bassline. This is a very common technique for bass players to use. Rather than everything being on the beat, we can introduce some 'swing' into the proceedings by bringing out some of the weaker beats in the bar. By giving these beats some sort of emphasis, the bassline starts to take on many of the attributes found in jazz's bottom end.

Ex 5.6

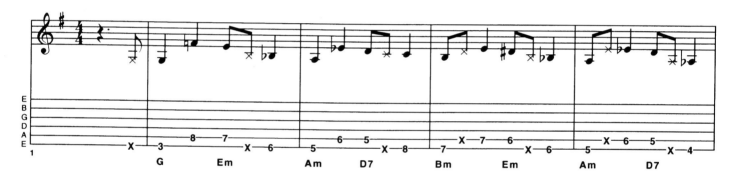

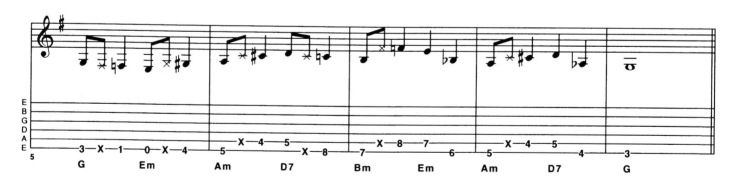

As a rhythmic variation, I think you'll agree that the last example really works well. But what happens if we transfer this 'offbeat' idea to the harmony part? If we use pretty much the same rhythmic emphasis, but this time use chords, the effect is quite dramatic.

Ex 5.7

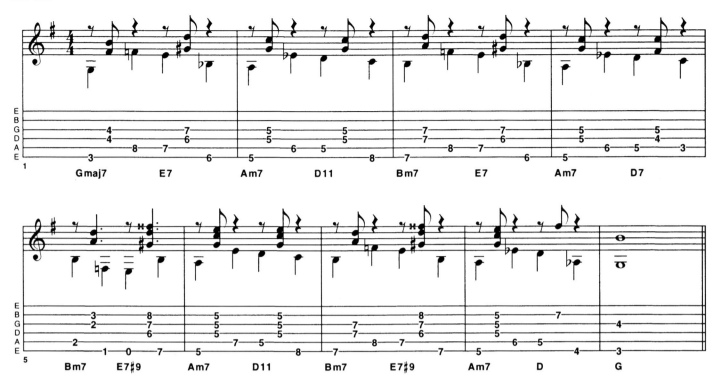

The chordal stabs are too short for the ear to really give them much harmonic significance. Their rhythmic effect is another thing, however. The offbeat quality of the harmony part gives the listener the impression that quite a lot is going on - and we haven't added any melody part so far.
Use your thumb to play all the bass notes, leaving your first and second fingers to play the stabs.

Thumb upstrokes
We look at the technique of using upstrokes with the thumb in the chapter 'Special Effects', but I thought I'd give you a glimpse here at how effective they can be in providing little rhythmic frills to a bass part.

Ex 5.8

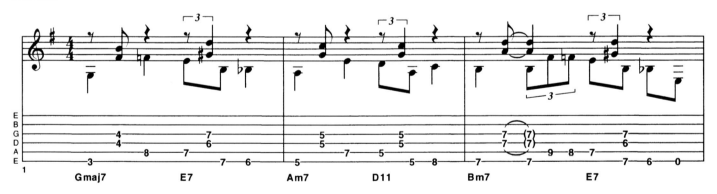

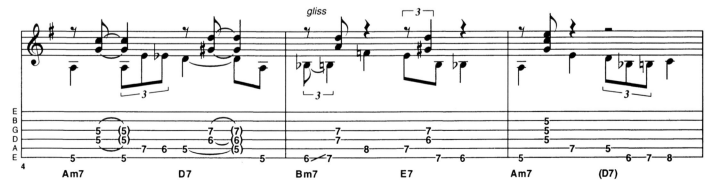

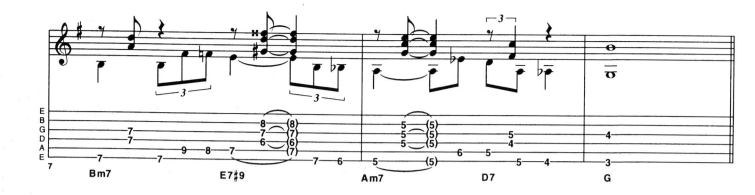

This really does start to make you sound like a one man rhythm section!

I have broken up the rhythm up a little, altering the straightforward 4/4 feel to produce a more interesting effect. Once again, I'd recommend that you familiarize yourself with the bass part first and put the stabs in later.

If the exact positioning of the chordal stabs looks a little daunting in the music notation, try listening to the CD and inserting a few at a time into your own version. I'm sure you'll soon get the hang of things.

Remember that all of the examples here will give you access to the idea of creating bass parts from a fairly basic level. To study further, I suggest you get hold of some transcriptions of chord melody playing and study the way the bass part has been put together. Remember also that there are no real rules to doing this sort of thing. Sometimes the absolute minimum movement in the bass is right for the song, whereas, at other times, you can allow things to get altogether more crazy.

RIGHT HAND TECHNIQUE

One thing a pianist has to cope with early on is right and left hand independence; they're nearly always playing different parts and so the brain has to adjust accordingly. But guitarists have an additional problem; not only have we got completely different functions to perform with our left and right hands, we also have to build in independence within the right hand fingers and thumb. Just something extra to think about, but it makes all the difference.

This section examines the vary basic principles of fingerstyle playing - essential to a contrapuntal chord melody style.

There has never really been an orthodoxy established for the right hand. No one's ever come out and said, 'this is the right way'. All we have to go on is the similarities between classical and 'popular' guitar technique in this respect. Hopefully, we're about to put that right.

For this lesson, we're going to be looking at the rights and wrongs of right hand position and how to ensure that your fingers have the best possible chance of working at maximum efficiency. After all, playing the guitar well is a difficult enough job and we don't want to make things unnecessarily hard for ourselves, do we?

I think that playing with flesh and nails as opposed to a pick actually sounds better, within the context of chord melody at any rate. It's something to do with that old thing about actually touching the string to produce the note instead of by proxy using a pick. But playing single lines fingerstyle has its limitations. Unless you are a top flight classical player like John Williams, attaining the necessary turn of speed for some of the up tempo material is very hard indeed. I have adopted a fingerstyle technique which is unorthodox, if viewed in the light of what a classical player would do. For instance, instead of using a regimented fingering like 'index - middle - index - middle' I tend to use whichever finger is handy at the time. It's a system that works for me, but I would recommend that you keep an open mind as you develop your own skills in this direction.

Naming the fingers

One of the more helpful things that classical technique can bestow upon us is the naming convention for the right hand fingers. It's not really been necessary to invent another one as things seem to run quite smoothly with the accepted convention in place. So here's what we've got:

Thumb = p
Index = i
Middle = m
Ring = a

You might have already guessed that these essentially lower case letters represent the Spanish names for the fingers, as opposed to random letters. If you scan some classical guitar music, you'll have come across this lettering convention before.

RIGHT HAND POSITION

© Carol Farnworth

This is my regular playing position, just in front of the neck pick-up.
Note little finger anchored to pick guard - it works for me, but don't copy it!

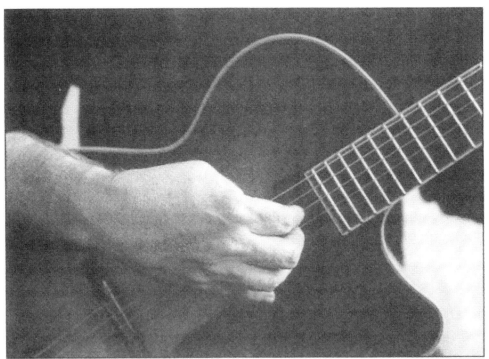

© Carol Farnworth

Note that my thumb is quite often behind my index finger. Once again, this is something
that works for me, but it might cause tension in your arm if you try it.

© Carol Farnworth

For playing single notes I haven't got a strict routine,
it's more a case of using whichever finger is available!

© Carol Farnworth

When I play bass parts, my thumb appears from behind my index finger. Notice that it's laid along
the string as opposed to the classical guitar regime of presenting the thumb at a 45° angle.

One of the first and most basic rules about right hand position is that you should try to eliminate tension in forearm, wrist, hand and fingers almost totally. Tensing up is your worst enemy for two main reasons: one, it decreases the hand's efficiency and two, it places you in danger of succumbing to an RSI type of complaint. We've all heard of tenosynovitis - swelling of a tendon due to repetitive movement - and it's something you really want to try and avoid as the only real cure is to stop playing for a while. So the best plan is to adopt a right hand position which will give your hand maximum flexibility and keep you out of hospital at the same time.

Because of the lack of a generally accepted 'correct' right hand position as far as rock, pop and jazz guitar is concerned, there are a variety of positions out there which defy all laws of feasibility by actually looking like they shouldn't work, but do. I'll deal with my own right hand position to begin with. If you study the pictures, you'll see that I anchor my right hand to the guitar's pickguard with my little finger. There is no mysterious reason why I do this, I just learned this way, that's all. If we go by the book, this hand position is actually 'wrong' by contemporary standards. Interestingly enough, anchoring the little finger was something that was quite acceptable in classical guitar technique a few hundred years ago, but not today.

In other words, I would recommend that you do not copy my right hand position. It works despite itself and it serves me adequately enough, but if you're new to fingerstyle guitar and want to adopt something that works, this isn't a particularly a good place to start. Get your own bad habits, don't imitate mine!

The classic touch

A good place to start is to look at the accepted classical guitar position. If you think about it, you're asking your hand to perform technique that covers pretty much the same area - that of playing melody, harmony and bass. The style is different, but the mechanics of the situation are very much the same, in other words.

The correct hand position for classical guitar means keeping the fingers of the hand as straight and uncramped as possible. Looking down from a player's point of view, the index finger and thumb should form something of an 'X'. This is merely to keep them out of each other's way when in action. I have to say at this point that my own thumb position is a little unconventional - unless you're a lute player from the 16th Century, that is. I'm told that my thumb position is very similar. I tend to keep my thumb under my index finger in more of a claw position. This is a technique favored by some country pickers - studying the photographs will help you see what I mean. If you're yet to establish a right hand thumb position, it's probably more sensible to follow convention, rather than mine. Clawing in the hand is looked on as being bad technique - and when you consider that I anchor my little finger, too...

When this position is transferred to the guitar strings, the fingers are very loosely assigned strings - I say 'loosely' because it's impossible to have too rigid a rule here as different fingerings will inevitably break every rule in the book eventually.

So, position your hand thus: the index finger (i) on the G string, the middle finger (m) on the B and the ring finger (a) on the top E. The thumb looks after the bass strings. Keep the fingers as straight as possible, don't let the wrist collapse, but don't arch it too high, either. Merely moving your fingers around will tell you that there is a lot of movement possible in this playing position and that's fine - we need optimum flexibility for approaching some of the music you're going to be playing.

Practical work

If you're trying to polish your fingerstyle skills it's best to work with a series of progressive exercises to build strength and dexterity rather than relying on pieces alone to hone this facility to perfection. If you're looking for a resource to put you on the right track with fingerstyle, you could do a lot worse than investigate a few classical guitar tutors who deal with the subject in a fair amount of detail. Some basic exercises would look like these. Think of this initial foray into the world of fingerpicking as orienteering - it's just so you can get your fingers used to sitting on the strings.

To begin with, adopt the finger position I spoke of a moment ago; thumb on the A, index on the G, middle on the B and ring on the top E and play the open strings thus.

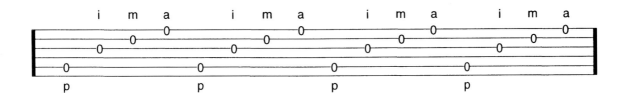

Exercise 2 is very similar, only it's in reverse; after the thumb plays, it's the top E string to be played first.

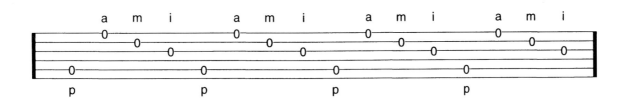

Both the above examples are not particularly musical - but it's a good thing to get both of them up and running before we give the left hand anything to do. This way around, you get to give your right hand all the attention it needs at this point.

Once you've got both Ex 1 and 2 running smoothly, take a look at Ex 3. It's only a C Major chord - nothing too demanding - but it will make things sound a little prettier.

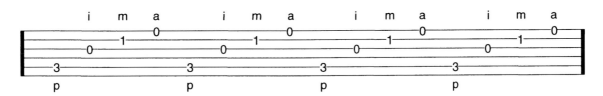

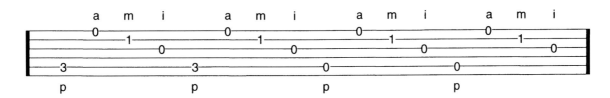

Both Ex 3 and 4 are essentially repeats of the first two, but a lot more musical.

Exercise 5 combines the two into one single movement - you're going over and back again. Take your time with this and don't accept any sloppy playing. It's got to flow evenly. If you have any problems, slow the exercise right down and try playing it with a metronome to keep it in check rhythmically.

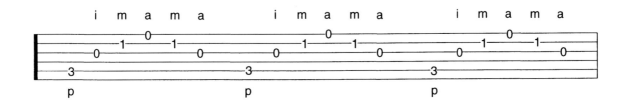

Exercise 6 throws another twist into the plot; this time, the thumb alternates between the A and D strings while the fingers carry out the work they've performed before. If these exercises tie you in knots, take your time, practice in short bursts so that you don't get frustrated with them and, above everything, have patience.

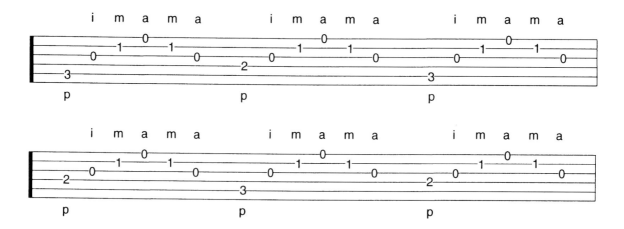

A final word of caution for fingerstyle exercises in general; if, at any time, you detect any discomfort in your wrist, fingers or hand, stop playing for a while and let the hand rest. It's learning new tricks and you're bound to feel a bit of resistance from muscles, etc, but don't overdo it.

Right hand tips:

1) Independence
As I've said before, the important thing with chord melody playing is to make sure that people can hear the melody. If played incorrectly, everything will come over as a blur and you won't be able to discern melody from accompaniment. It's not a thing that comes naturally - you have to work on the independence of the right hand fingers before you stand any real chance of a good result. If I was to simplify the process, I would say that all that has to happen is that the fingers you assign to the task of playing the melody as opposed to the accompaniment have to hit the strings harder. We call this 'internal dynamics'. Make an exercise out of it on an easy chord series and practice bringing out different notes by plucking harder with the relevant fingers. Gradually, you'll find that you can control the dynamics of what you play far more easily with the effect that the melody will ring clear above the chords or bass line that supports it.

2) Syncopation
Syncopation with the right hand means that your thumb and index finger (for instance) might be playing a different timing or rhythmic pattern from the rest of your fingers. Just think of some of the ragtime piano pieces by Scott Joplin and you'll know what I mean. In its simplest form, syncopation could just be the art of playing a 4/4 bass part against some off-beat chordal stabs with the fingers. If this sort of thing is a problem then it's best to try to solve it with some technical exercises, rather than by trying to play a piece which incorporates it 'from cold'. Even if you managed to work your way through a transcription and incorporated all the syncopation, it's likely that the end result would be that you could play this piece well, but the same problem would dog you when you try to play anything else like it. Always try to isolate these areas that need development and deal with them in a purely businesslike, technical way. By doing this, you are allowing the technical side of your musicianship to develop; it will become a means by which you can access lots of different areas of music and it's important that you consider it as pure technique and not associate it with a single particular piece.

To train your right hand to play syncopation, you'll need to start with a 4/4 rhythm, using the three right hand fingers (index, middle and ring) with your thumb plucking the strings simultaneously. Then try alternating between thumb and fingers, gradually introducing 'off beats' along the way. Eventually, it will become second nature and you won't even have to think about it. But, like everything we learn, the process has to be fully in the head before it can start to feel natural (think about the first time you drove a car or rode a bicycle).

In classical guitar, it's not uncommon for a player to work out a fingering for his right hand before even delving into the piece itself with both. You can practice right hand fingerings on open strings so that your concentration is more focused than it would be if you had both hands to worry about at once. Then, once the right hand knows what it's doing, you can bring in the other hand. Do this with the arpeggios one at a time and you're bound to get results.

It's just like mastering any synchronized movement - patting your head while rubbing your tummy is a good example. It's fearsomely difficult when you first try it, but a bit of practice makes it easier and easier.

It's a question of the fingers of the right hand being assigned different jobs; I tend to assign my ring finger for melody work, the index and middle for 'rhythm' and keep the thumb for playing the bass. This, of course, is just a general rule which I break every time I pick up a guitar, but it might serve as a guide if you want to work on your fingerstyle technique.

3) Ironing out bad habits

Always deal with blind spots in isolation. There is nothing to be gained from persisting with bad technique. Take a good look at where any weaknesses lie in your playing and make plans to put things right. Don't keep playing the same old pieces time and time again with the same old errors all the way through them. The only way to put things right is to dig down to the foundations of your playing and try to track down where the problems are and put some sort of practice routine in place to deal with them. Go back to basics every so often and take a long cold look at your technique and see if there's anything there which doesn't work - it's well worth the effort.

4) Make sure you're playing with a full deck

Even hardened fingerstylists can find that the ring finger lies fallow. The only way to combat this is to try to introduce the ring finger into the action slowly, a little at a time. Work out some exercises where you deliberately use this finger more and more. This is a good way to extend your range as a musician, by literally increasing the power of your right hand.

LEFT HAND TECHNIQUE

Looking at some of the pictures included in this chapter should give you a good idea of my own left hand position. I tend to keep my first - or index - finger in such a position where it is always ready to place a barre. That is, unless I'm playing single lines, of course. I find it enables me to move between chord shapes with greater ease. I tend not to use big stretches, too - although occasionally this can't be avoided. It's not true that all jazz guitar chords call for acts of extreme gymnastics on behalf of your fretting hand, but some gentle stretching exercises during your practice routine wouldn't come amiss.

During the early introduction to jazz chord voicings, you might find that even the more modest looking variations give the fingers some trouble. Forming part barres with the second or third fingers is a well known stumbling block for many guitarists, but these hurdles are easily overcome if they receive their due amount of practice.

Once again, I'd recommend that you explore chord variations and inversions by playing through songs, rather than blindly studying a chord book. If your experiments call for some unfamiliar positions, then so much the better - this is the way we all learn. It's a more natural way than trying to commit chord forms to memory like you're learning some laws of physics.

Underhand practices

Let's look at a few statistics for a moment. The guitar has approximately half the range of the piano, in terms of notes. This means that the best we can expect is marginally less than four octaves of musical range available to us as musicians. Some rock guitars have 24 fret necks, giving them the full four octave range, whereas jazz archtops are more likely to clock in at 20 frets or so, giving us a grand total of 3.7 octaves to play with.

Now, consider what exactly lies under your hand on the guitar neck at any one time. If you place your first finger on, say, the fifth fret and let the rest of your fingers fall naturally on the neck so that your little finger is on the eighth fret, you'd be surprised at just how much of the guitar's full range you've got covered. In actual fact, you've got two and a quarter octaves available to you in this position - more than half the instrument's full range! So you might see from this statistic that wild position changes and inhuman stretches need not be everyday events, by any means. In fact, such movements are usually acknowledging the instrument's limitations - let me explain.

Some chord voicings call for close harmony, which means that you're dealing with intervals like seconds, and these don't fall naturally under the fingers on the guitar. However, they do sound good and so we have to make the odd stretch here and there to accommodate them. Think about it; the guitar is tuned in fourths and so playing the notes C and C♯ from the same octave together in a chord voicing is going to provide you with some quite athletic fingering. If you were to play the C at the first fret on the B string, the nearest C♯ is on the sixth fret on the G string. Try it, it's quite a stretch (and I realize it doesn't sound fantastic either, this is just an experiment). This is a fairly extreme example, but you'll meet the same problem when you try to voice other close intervals. It's certainly a statistic which is worth bearing in mind when you're working out some arrangements in the early stages. People tell me that I don't use too many hand position changes when I play - this is one of the reasons why.

Biology for guitarists

The most important thing to remember, if you're moving into uncharted territory with chord voicings is that you're asking the hand to do things it wasn't designed to do. Certain muscles that were quite happily dormant before you decided to play guitar are in for a tough time while they develop the necessary strength and flexibility to cope with some of the things you're asking them to do. To this end, take things easy and don't try to rush anything. These things take time and so you'll have to tell yourself that you're going to deal with the frustration of not being able to do certain things on the guitar until you've spent a certain amount of time pumping iron.

Do some exercises that will aid the development of your hands - scales, etc - and remember to warm up before each practice session. This is important as guitarists can end up with repetitive strain injury if things are pushed too hard too fast. Patience is your main ally here. But the thing that will help your hands become accustomed to the rigours of guitar life more than anything is playing.

I use a lot of barre chords in my playing and so my index finger is nearly always ready to lay a barre across the fretboard... (see pic. 2)

This is the same chord as in pic. 1 with the barre in place.

With the playing position I use, which is standing up with the guitar fairly high, you rarely see my thumb over the top of the neck - although sometimes it will come forward to hold down a bass note which would otherwise be out of reach.

My left arm is totally relaxed when I play with the forearm and elbow in a natural position. This is important in order to eliminate tension.

Phrasing

Non-wind instruments like the guitar often suffer from unnatural sounding phrasing. Because we never need to take a breath between phrases like a sax player does, the resulting music tends to be tumultuous and suffocating. It's a good idea for guitarists to learn how to 'breathe' in their playing. Singing or humming melodies yourself is a good way of learning the technique – the great jazz pianist and teacher Lennie Tristano used to encourage his pupils to sing entire solos to take their focus away from the instrument and let the music have its own life inside their heads. One of the main benefits from singing along as you play is that it encourages you to phrase naturally because you have to pause for breath occasionally. Wind instrument players have the advantage there, but guitarists are notorious for not leaving any space in their playing.

Good phrasing is like speaking; we leave natural gaps and pauses, we add emphasis to certain words and everything has a sort of natural flow to it. You should try to aim for the same fluency when you play. The way you phrase will be your own personal signature, just like your natural speech pattern.

Another thing that inspired me was how vocalists treat melody - Frank Sinatra was a master of phrasing. Take a listen and hear how he holds back notes or pushes the beat on some phrases and try to use that kind of idea in your own playing. It can make an awful lot of difference to even the slightest melody.

Rephrasing a melody

One of the first steps towards understanding the principles involved in jazz phrasing is to learn to rephrase a melody. Try holding on to notes for longer than their allotted time value or adjusting the rhythm another way. It's very difficult to teach someone how to phrase because it's such an individual thing; everyone has their own way of doing it.

When I play, I tend to let the timing of the piece remain very 'free' - that is to say that it's not strict four to the bar. When my solo pieces are transcribed, quite often they have been 'quantized' - in other words, they have been copied out in such a way that they 'fit' rhythmically speaking and so, in a way, you could say that what you see on paper isn't quite what I have actually played. I believe that a 'free form' approach sounds better and lets the music create its own space. It's more dramatic, too, in the way that it allows you to stretch things - the music rises and falls naturally. But things have to remain coherent and so it's better to use a transcription as a guide rhythmically and then use your own creativity to let it flow as you see fit.

Timing is not something that you can learn to do with a stopwatch, it's more of a 'feel' thing and listening to different players interpret tunes will give you some idea of what I mean. The main idea is to create space – don't be in a rush to fill every conceivable space, more often than not it's what you leave out which makes this type of playing more effective.

Listen to the great jazz pianists Bill Evans and Keith Jarret - they are supreme masters of phrasing, in my opinion.

Rhythm

Nobody ever asks about rhythm - it's one of the neglected areas of learning an instrument. And yet a simple process of being made rhythmically aware can make all the difference.

Good rhythm comes from the inside; you've got to be able to feel the pulse of the music at all times. It's a good idea to tap your foot along with a metronome because this means that your body is learning to feel rhythm - it's not just something you're listening to on the outside.

Rhythm is essential when you're playing with other musicians, too. It's your inner sense that helps you keep in sync with everything else going on around you and a musician who is out of tune with his sense of rhythm sticks out like a badly tuned instrument.

Altering a tune's basic rhythm

Rhythm can play a vital part of your arranging skills. One of the more straightforward ways of presenting a familiar tune in an unfamiliar way is to alter its rhythmic structure. For instance, in its original form, 'My Funny Valentine' is a slow ballad and this is usually the treatment that singers and instrumentalists have given it over the years. However, I decided to give the tune an altogether different treatment and rearrange it as a bossa nova. When I play it live, I often play it quite fast.

It's amazing what you can do to a tune just by altering its rhythmic nature - or basic 'groove'. It means that, in many cases, the melody is presented in a completely new light for your audience and it opens up a lot of possibilities for you as a performer, too.

Jazz waltzing

One word of caution here; when jazz musicians talk about a waltz, they're quite likely referring to a 'jazz waltz'.

Fundamentally, the difference between a straight and jazz waltz shows up in the time signature. The difference is probably more profound than you would think. A lot of jazz waltzes tend to be in 6/8, that time signature is actually based on two beats to the bar as opposed to 3/4's more waltz-like three. It's just that, in 6/8, each beat is a triplet, which gives it a slight 'three' feel.

TONE

Like rhythm, tone is another neglected area, and yet it is inherent to the musician's own 'voice' on his instrument.

Quite often, when a guitarist thinks about tone, he will think of the rotary control on either his guitar or amplifier. This is all well and good (and yet how many players actually use their guitar's tone controls?) but it's not anywhere near the full story. The guitar, like any stringed instrument, has a natural tonal range, in much the same way as it has a dynamic range - you can control your guitar's volume without even touching the volume control.

The great jazz guitarist Johnny Smith never altered his volume control once he'd set it for a performance; all his dynamics came from his hands.

Dynamic range

Music demands contrast and it's probably one of the most simple characteristics to introduce to your playing. Very basic physics tells us that the harder you pluck a string, the more volume it produces and yet so many guitar students tend to ignore this and play at a single dynamic level. It's a simple experiment to do; play a chord on your guitar as quietly as you can. Then, pluck the chord with the fingers with increasing force until it's about as loud as it will go. Now you have explored the dynamic range of your instrument (it varies from guitar to guitar). In practice, you'll be playing at roughly 80% of the full range, giving you the chance to introduce quite dramatic highs and lows into your playing.

Tonal range

Classical guitarists are well aware of the two main tonal extremes on their guitars; plucking near the bridge produces a bright, almost metallic tone or timbre. Plucking nearer the neck produces a warm, sweet sound. With this in mind, it is possible to vary the tonal properties of the music they play to great effect. Introduce variations in dynamic range and you can see that there is an awful lot you can do to control your sound - and not a volume or tone control in sight!

On an archtop guitar, the pick-up of choice for many of the traditionalists is the neck or 'rhythm' pick-up, the bridge offering perhaps too much brightness. I solved this dilemma on my own signature model in a unique way (see chapter 'Guitar Design') but I also control the tone and dynamic range of my guitar using the methods described above.

You need to fully explore the dynamic and tonal range of your guitar. When I recorded 'Tone Poems II' with David Grisman and the Chinery Guitar Collection with Steve Howe, I played over 100 vintage guitars. The first thing I did when I was handed a guitar for the first time was to find the guitar's 'sweet spot'. That is, the exact spot to strike the strings which gave the guitar its maximum response and sound its best. Once you know where that is, then you have a good understanding of that particular guitar's strengths and weaknesses. Finding the sweet spot is something I have always done naturally, without even thinking about it, but it's a skill that can be developed very quickly and easily. Play around with your guitar; play loud and soft at different points. Only then will you be able to fully realize exactly what your instrument is capable of.

SPECIAL EFFECTS

You don't need me to tell you that jazz guitar is very unlike rock guitar in terms of sheer flamboyance. But it's interesting to note that players like Tal Farlow were into 'tapping', or fretting notes with the right hand, before the acknowledged pioneer of this particular art, Edward Van Halen, was born! Subtlety, though, is the watchword here. Most of jazz guitar's 'special effects' are there for solid musical reasons which extend some sort of musical facility that wouldn't otherwise be available.

Detuning the bass

Not really anything new as far as guitar is concerned - acoustic players have made a career out of altered tunings. We're only talking about the bass string.

In chord melody playing, you're playing your own bass part and sometimes it's good to accentuate this by dropping the low E even lower. The most extreme example of this from my own repertoire is in a song called 'Song for Alex' where I dropped the bass string to a low A - an octave lower than the fifth string - and introduced the bass part during the second verse. I know of at least one person who thought there must be a double bass player off stage somewhere when I performed the tune live. Someone else at a live performance had made up their mind that I must have used MIDI on my two bass strings. I didn't - dropping the bass string was far more simple!

On other occasions, I drop the tuning of my bass string at the end of a piece. This either works or it doesn't, it's a little hit or miss. But it's a good way of finishing a piece.

Thumbs Up

Back in the chapter on basslines, we looked very briefly at my technique of using upstrokes with my thumb. This can be a very effective rhythmic idea to introduce into a bass part and the technique is not such a hard one to master. Obviously, the convention is to use downstrokes with the thumb and so you are going to have to change slightly the way you think about using your thumb. It's just a question of training the thumb to sound the string with an upwards movement - oh, and it helps if you have something of a thumbnail.

Here's a solo example of the thumb being used in this way.

Ex 6.1

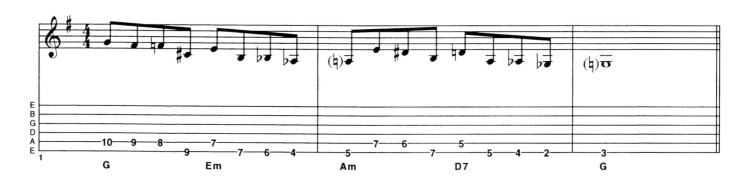

I'm emphasizing the notes on the recording a little more than I would do in a performance. This is to let you hear where they fall in the bar more clearly.

Here's the same idea again, but this time with some harmony on top to help place everything in its proper context.

Ex 6.2

There is a fair amount of syncopation going on in this last example and playing it is going to present your right hand with quite a challenge. So take things slowly and practice it in parts if you have to. Remember that this is only one idea of how a slightly modified technique can take your playing into new areas.

Using upstrokes with the thumb isn't necessarily to facilitate speed, it's more concerned with rhythm - a percussive effect - as these upstrokes tend to be representative of offbeats that you hear double bass players insert into a swing bass part.

Artificial harmonics

These are the 'harplike' harmonics you hear which seem to be interspersed with ordinary chords. You may be familiar with the technique of sounding a harmonic using solely the right hand: stop the string 12 frets higher than any fretted note being held down by the left hand using your index finger. Then, use the right hand middle finger to sound the harmonic. Then, alternate the artificial harmonic with a straightforward plucked note. Here's what it sounds like on open strings:

Ex 6.3

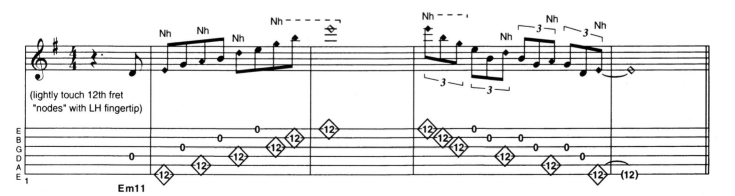

This technique really comes into its own when you use it on chords. First of all, you fret a chord with the left hand and play artificial harmonics 12 frets higher, tracing out the shape of the chord with the right hand. Once everything is working properly here, you can bring in the actual notes of the chord alternatively. Use the right hand thumb to pluck the notes whilst the ring finger and index finger play the artificial harmonics every other note. Here are a couple of examples:

Exs 6.4 & 6.5

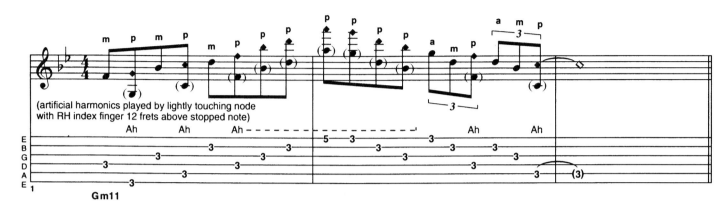

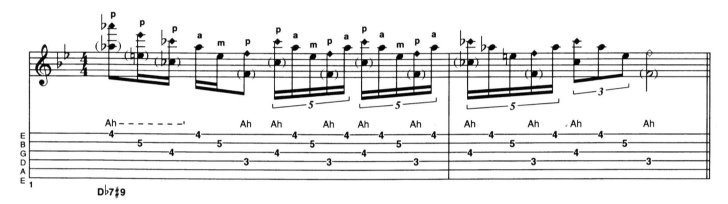

I don't claim to be an expert of this technique and use it very sparingly. To hear the real masters of artificial harmonics, check out Bireli Lagrene, Ted Greene and Tommy Emmanuel.

It's not easy, but once you get the basic mechanics of the technique up and running you can begin to bring it up to speed and eventually, natural notes merge into artificial harmonics to give this very special effect.

THE 'DANNY BOY' VARIATIONS

In this chapter, I'm going to take a tune from a very basic state right up to performance level to help you see more clearly the process of putting together a chord melody arrangement. Experience has taught me that it's no good doing this sort of thing on a well weathered jazz standard. There are too many versions available already in the jazz mainstream and these will invariably influence you and lead you away from the simple path we need to be upon. Once, when I was writing for the UK's Guitarist magazine, David Mead and I put together a series of variations on the nursery rhyme 'Baa Baa Black Sheep' (called 'Baa Baa Be-Bop Sheep') and this idea became almost ridiculously successful - I still get asked about it at gigs today! The thing was that the tune was one that nearly everyone knew and, more importantly, didn't associate with jazz. In this respect, they were able to see more clearly how the process of arrangement works, without being prejudiced by anything they'd heard previously.

For this book, we've decided to use the famous song 'Danny Boy', or 'Londonderry Air', if you prefer. I hope this will have the same sort of appeal and effect, allowing you to take a beautiful melody and arrange it in different ways.

Where to start?

There are many things that will influence a tune's arrangement. Sometimes it might be something as simple as the way you hear a particular song in your head. A familiar melody line played in a slightly different style, for instance. Or you could be stringing a few chords together on your guitar during a practice session and find that they alone are enough to suggest an arrangement idea for a melody. But there are other factors to be considered, too. Lyrics should have an influence on an arrangement of a tune one way or another. You could choose to take a melancholy love song and turn it into an up-tempo bop, but would it really suit the mood of the tune? Should you really render a sprightly tune like 'Top Hat, White Tie And Tails' as a slow, moody ballad? Of course, in the end, it's up to you. Duke Ellington is on record as saying that jazz is the music of surprise and so you might want to turn these things around occasionally. But it is always worth keeping a song's lyrical content in mind when attempting an arrangement.

Obviously, the most important thing to consider in any arrangement is the melody. Arranging a tune with dense clusters of harmony is all well and good, but is the melody still recognizable? If it isn't, you're possibly going to alienate your audience - and you need them on your side.

Setting up a tune

They say that first impressions count for an awful lot and that is certainly true of intros to chord melody pieces. Here, it is your job to set the scene for the piece you are about to play; create the proper atmosphere and draw your audience in to the main body of the song. It's a time when you can be at your most creative, too; imagine - you've got at least eight bars in which you can let your creativity run riot.

If you take a listen to some of the songs written during the 30s and 40s, it was common practice to have a fairly long introduction before the 'refrain'. Now, it tends to be just the refrain that we know, the introductions having fallen into disuse - a shame, in my opinion. However, if you check out some of the Ella Fitzgerald recordings of Gershwin, you'll be surprised to hear how very familiar tunes have quite startlingly unfamiliar introductions. Check out songs like 'I Got Rhythm' or 'A Foggy Day' and you'll see what I mean.

So, by offering our audience an introduction to a familiar tune, we are keeping up a long-standing tradition - despite the fact we might not be playing the composer's original idea.

So how do we come about 'inventing' an introduction? Well, there are no rules; you don't have to start in the same key as the song you're about to play - in fact, it's probably as well that you don't. Keep the audience guessing until they hear those first familiar melody notes. Sometimes, the simple ploy of repeating an idea at various places on the fretboard can have the desired effect - try it; I think you'll see what I mean. Here's an example of an intro I might use to set up 'Danny Boy':

Ex 7.1

Hopefully, you'll be able to see how that particular example was able to suggest the melody of 'Danny Boy' without actually quoting from it. You don't want to give away too much too soon, remember.

Of course, there are many different ways to introduce a song and you really can afford to let your imagination run free on this point. An effective idea might come from just a couple of chords, like this:

Ex 7.2

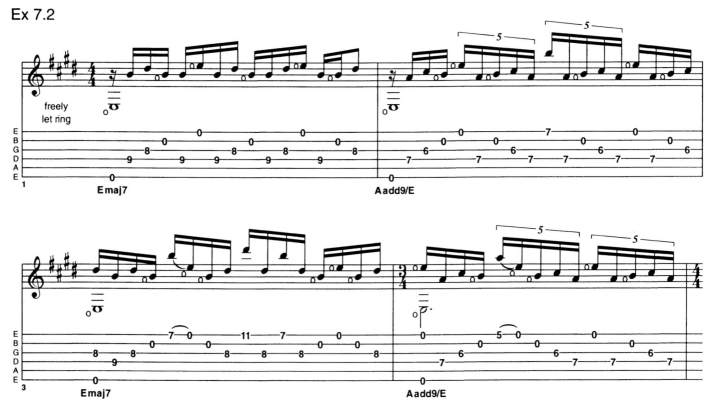

In this example, I dressed the chords up a little, but to me they sound like they're asking a question - 'what's coming next?' - and hopefully the melody is going to provide the answer. Remember, you're trying to arouse your audience's curiosity, get them interested in the song.

Influences on a tune
Of course, there are many factors to take into account when you're arranging a tune for performance and so I thought it would be worthwhile to consider a few of them before we leap headlong into 'Danny Boy'.

Tempo
Sometimes, you'll tackle a piece which was originally written for big band and, despite the fact that we've only got six strings at our disposal, with a little effort we can summon up the style and feel of a large 'jazz orchestra'.

When faced with this particular challenge myself, I try to include as many moving parts within the tune's basic melody. This is done to imitate the way the different instruments of a big band would play different sections of the arrangement in counterpoint. I sometimes - as in the case of Neil Hefti's 'Li'l Darlin' for instance - take the tempo right down and play very slightly behind the beat. This makes the tune sound 'large' - it literally acquires more weight in this way. The only downside is that slower tempos are invariably harder to play. It's a fact that often surprises newcomers to the instrument, but it's true; playing in time at slower tempos is more difficult. If you need proof, set your metronome to about 40-60 beats per minute and play a simple eighth note rhythm. Now increase the setting to 100 BPM - which was easier to maintain over the period of a minute?

I suppose that the easiest way to become familiar with a big band sound is to take some time out to listen to people like Count Basie and Duke Ellington. Take note how the melody is arranged between all the different instruments, but listen especially to the overall 'feel'. This is the mysterious and elusive element that we are trying to capture with this particular piece. I learned an awful lot about arranging from big band recordings and try to bring what I have learned to everything I do on the guitar.

I learned a lot from hearing some of the orchestrations by Nelson Riddle. Nelson was a huge influence on my formative years and I had the pleasure of working with him shortly before he died. I'd advise any student of chord melody guitar to seek out some of his recordings - you might not have a full orchestra at your disposal, but all the basic principles of great arranging are right there for you.

Melody
As I've said so many times, the most important thing to do when tackling an arrangement is to make sure the melody is well defined. If you're not sure of the melody - and you should know it so well that you can hum it without mistakes - check out the original. So many people say they don't like jazz because there's too much playing and too few tunes and so this simple bit of research will stand you in very good stead on the bandstand.

As far as bringing out the melody within the arrangement is concerned, the only technical trick you have to learn on the guitar is the ability to play louder with some fingers than others. That is to say, you give the melody preference over the harmony. It might sound like a tall order to bring this off, but it's standard practice amongst classical guitarists who have to learn how to make the melody of a piece stand out from the accompaniment. The technique is easier to describe than to do, perhaps, but isolating the technique and giving it special attention when you practice should begin to make the task easier after a while.

First, learn the tune

If you really know how a tune sits on your fretboard, then you can improvise more efficiently. This is even more important if you are yet to become a sure-footed jazz improviser because you will always have the melody there as a kind of 'handrail' to guide you up the somewhat rickety steps of jazz harmony. Remember that a melody will always have a snug relationship with its harmony and will always accommodate any little harmonic 'surprises' perfectly. Melody is important from an audience point of view, too. It's their major reference point.

But how do you go about turning a melody into something that resembles jazz? I believe it all begins with learning to vary the melody to begin with. Played at a moderate to slow tempo, the melody has a lot of gaps in it where nothing is happening and these are the ideal spaces to fill with a couple of ideas of your own. Start off by playing a couple of notes which you know are in the melody already in these spaces - even a random selection should sound OK. But we don't want to keep this as a 'shot in the dark' process - that's not how the trick works at all. You have to learn to hear which notes you want to play and find them on the fretboard instantaneously. If this sounds impossible to you, then I can assure you that it sounds impossible to everyone at first, so don't give up.

Once you have successfully played a couple of melody notes in the melodic gaps, it might be time to explore some chromatic tones. This gives everything its 'jazz' sound, but it needs to be used with caution at first. There's nothing worse than a bad note in a good place and so a considerable amount of trial and error is going to have to take place while you practice before you begin getting the trick right every time. If two notes in the melody are a tone (three inclusive frets) apart, see what they sound like with that middle note filled in. Try to arrange it so that you play the weaker chromatic tone on an offbeat if possible. The important notes need to be on the important beats of the bar.

I've said many times before that I would rather teach a method where students are encouraged to use their ears from the word go, rather than build up a vocabulary of relative chords and spend all their time applying a mathematical formula while they play. Experiment with patience - you're bound to be rewarded.

Less is more

When you've spent a lot of time fusing together the elements of melody, harmony and bass, the chances are that your arrangement might sound too dense. Many students who try to put together chord melody pieces in their initial stages find that they've literally tried too hard. You don't have to harmonize every single note of a melody.

Most of the time, it sounds like there is more going on in one of my solo arrangements than there actually is. It sounds like there are multiple parts playing together, when most of the time, it's really an illusion. It's also a trick that classical guitar players pull off all the time. Think of a piece of Baroque guitar music, many of these have two parts - sometimes three - happening simultaneously and yet many are quite straightforward in their execution.

Set up a groove

The basic groove is the most important part of many pieces because it's got to hang in the background and support everything you do on top. Even though it's not always played, your audience will be aware of its presence - some will even swear that you played it all the way through if you do the job right. It's the musical equivalent of 'find the lady' only this time it's the speed of the hand that deceives the ear.

If you listen to some of the more up tempo or groove orientated pieces I've recorded in the past, check out how I nearly always refer back to the song's groove in between the licks on top. This is another important device which will hold up in any chord melody playing. But, more importantly, I will occasionally refer directly to the harmony of the piece in order to ensure that the listener keeps in touch. You have to act as guide in this way because you know the tune in an almost entirely different way to your listener. You see it as notes and chords, themes and variations - whereas, a lot of the time, your audience sees it as something pretty to sing in the shower. So you have to grab the audience's hand every so often and help them through the areas where the tune lapses into improvisation - without the security of the melody in place, they could easily become lost and there's no quicker way to ruin someone's enjoyment of music.

As far as swapping between chords and solo ideas with the right hand, we find ourselves looking again at the basic principles of fingerstyle. If you play with your fingers then you'll find yourself playing the licks with RH fingers one and two, almost in the same way that a classical guitarist would. For me, there's not really a system; a lot of players ask me if I play using alternate fingers, but, after thinking about it for a long time, I can honestly say that I just use whichever finger is handy at the time.

Danny Boy

Londonderry Air, the tune on which Danny Boy is based, was first published in 1855 and nearly 150 years later it's still going strong.

The melody for 'Danny Boy' is so strong and well known, I felt that I didn't want to clutter it with a lot of unnecessary arrangement. When you've got a melody which is this strong, it's unwise to mess too much with it - a case of 'if it ain't broke, don't fix it'. I tried several keys before settling on E major; the melody seemed to fit the fretboard far better in E for some reason.

Another thing I've tried to avoid is laboring a beautiful melody with unnecessary 'jazz' voicings. A lot of people make the mistake of thinking that, just because they are playing in a jazz context, they have to dress every single chord up with extended dominant sevenths and so on. I think this tune in particular has got so much of a life of its own that it would be wrong to impose too much of a foreign style on it - it started as a folk tune, after all.

From a technical standpoint, watch the notation closely. There's nothing too much to worry about, but we will be using a fair amount of the fretboard, so watch out for those position changes, barres and so on.

Try to put as much feeling into this piece as you can. It really doesn't matter whether you play it at a medium tempo or dead slow; if the feeling's there, the piece will stand up for itself.

The first version I've recorded is the very basic chords with the melody line on top. Use this version as basic orienteering and remember to make sure that you learn both melody and harmony thoroughly, otherwise little of what follows will make any sense to you.

The next version is slightly more 'arranged'. This is really the first step away from the basic 'chords with melody' approach. The harmony part contains more arpeggiation and I'm allowing some variations on the melody to creep through every so often. The most important thing is that the melody still has a life of its own; the harmony part isn't intruding in any way and yet there is just enough there to give the melody support.

Danny Boy Variations Ex 4

Study both arrangements together and take note of how the second version evolves from the first. Next, I'm going to add an intro and play a version which would be a 'performance version'.

Ex 7.5

Danny Boy Variations Ex 5

You'll notice here how I've incorporated some of the techniques we've been looking at already and one of the original 'intro' sections.

Also, I've put in the occasional 'jazz' chord voicing and even the odd bluesy fill, but I've kept these to a minimum. The melody is still this version's strongest feature.

A further variation we can make is in the actual style of 'Danny Boy'. So far, I've played it pretty much as written; a beautiful meandering ballad. But what happens if we introduce a rhythmic element to it and try to give it a bit of a groove? So, for the next version, I've introduced a kind of bossa nova feel to the tune. I've also taken a few more liberties with both melody and harmony...

Ex 7.6   **Danny Boy Variations Ex 6**

69

Continuing the theme of rhythmic variations, the next version has a distinct 'swing' feel to it, plus a few more 'jazz' chord voicings in the harmony.

7.7   **Danny Boy Variations Ex 7**

There is a lot of work for you to do in the previous few examples, but I hope they illustrate the process whereby a tune can be turned into a satisfying chord melody piece. Study the music and tablature and form your own conclusions; I can assure you that when I play I'm not employing any formula, I'm just playing what I hear in my head. So it's up to you to analyze the music in this book and learn from it in your own way. This way you will be best prepared to make your own arrangements in your own unique style. Good luck!

BHAI BHAI BLUES

I hope the time you have spent with this book has been of benefit to you and that your studies will continue well into the future.

I thought it was appropriate to leave you with a blues. I'm not going to write up extensive notes as to its key, content, choice of chord inversions, scales or rhythmic patterns - all of these things are there for you to unravel in the music below. Remember to experiment with everything you have learned, form your own conclusions and, most of all, play it your way!

Ex 8.1

Bhai Bhai Blues

74

77

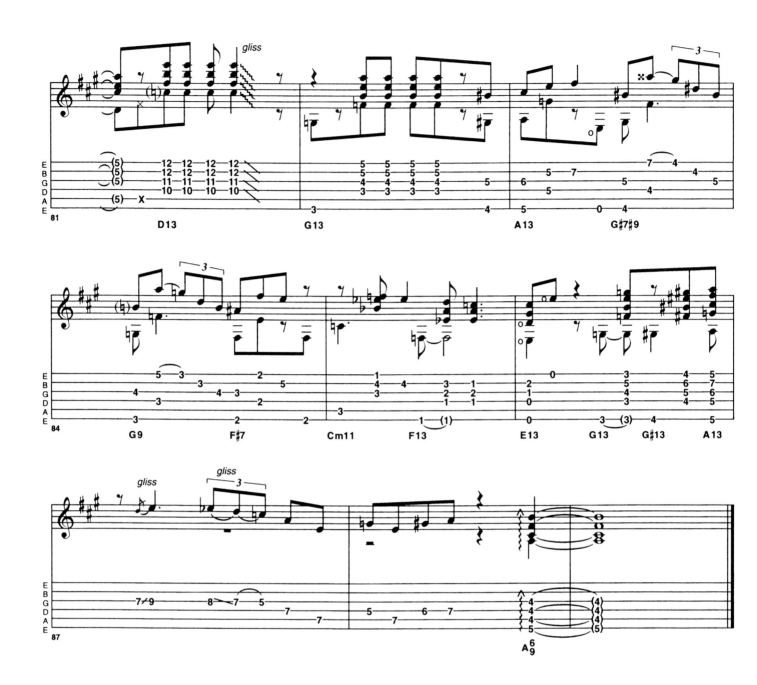

Guitar Design

Since I started playing, I've had a number of guitars by various makers, including Framus, Guild, Barker, Gibson and Yamaha. Over the years, I've formed my own ideas about what I want from a guitar. Obviously, my style makes certain demands on an instrument and it's a rare instrument that can deal with all my various foibles as a player.

Back in 1998, all the good bits of design I've experienced in the past were decanted into the instrument I'm playing at the moment which is my own signature model, The Martin Taylor Artistry, made by luthier Mike Vanden who lives and works in north west Scotland.

Guitar

The jazz world is a bit conservative. I thought it was time for something a bit different: a modern jazz guitar which still keeps some of the classic look of its forebears. The full-bodied jazz guitar is an American invention. I wanted to give this guitar something of a European look and so I had the cutaway designed more in the Macaferri tradition and this is mirrored in the design of the headstock. For a detailed look at The Artistry, I'll hand you over to David Mead's original review which was published in the UK's Guitarist magazine in November 1999.

The guitar's overall shape evolved after hours of Martin and Mike gradually refining a full scale drawing, pinned to the workshop wall. It's in keeping with the classic, full-bodied jazzer lines of yore, but with enough of a modern, unconventional edge.

It's immediately apparent, too, that we are dealing with a guitar where the design ethic was clearly to build a full bodied jazz instrument from the point of view of an acoustic guitar. In that respect, the electrical side of The Artistry isn't that obvious. Mini pots and a microscopic toggle switch nestle on the pick guard and the woody neck pick-up and bridge piezo realize a level of discreetness that most major politicians could only dream of.

The Artistry's top is made from bookmatched spruce. Back, sides and neck are maple, with ebony the wood of choice for peg head veneer, fingerboard, bridge and tailpiece. The nut is fashioned from bone, while the truss rod cover and side markers are made from Tahiti pearl - a very exotic, almost metallic looking substance which makes the truss rod cover look holographic under certain lighting conditions. The rest of The Artistry's inlay is mother of pearl. The neck fits snugly in the hand, which is good when you consider it was designed to fit Martin's and not mine. Martin was very specific about the neck width; after all, playing fingerstyle requires arguably more from a fretboard, specifically at the nut end. To meet these requirements, The Artistry clocks in at 44 mm at

the nut, broadening out to 56 mm at the 14th fret. It was Martin's idea, too, that the fingerboard should be free of the usual markers, in keeping with the instrument's overall classy, almost understated look.

Another of Martin's specific requests was that the guitar responds more like an acoustic than an electric. This is the eternal conundrum for guitar makers trying to build a 'best of both worlds' instrument and usually sacrifices have to be made. How many times have you picked up an electro-acoustic only to find that it's more one way then the other? Happily, in the case of The Artistry, it responds exactly like a high grade acoustic instrument and the electrics don't interfere. The combination of the Mimesis and the piezo bridge pick-ups bring out the very best and most versatile of electric voices

The controls on the guitar's pick guard comprise a blend rotary - for mixing the two pick-up sounds - and volume. The mini toggle switch is a rather clever affair, too. Martin's playing style calls for both fingerstyle and plectrum and this switch accommodates the attack differential. Fingers are softer than plastic and so a flick of the switch produces a 4 dB cut around the 2-3 kHz audio range. It's neat, clever and simple, and it's another idiosyncrasy deftly dealt with by Mike Vanden.

The guitar's active electrics are governed by two separate pre-amps: one for the Mimesis, one for the piezo. Sensibly enough, the power comes from two readily available six volt lithium cells. The cells have a minimum lifespan of a hundred hours and are activated when the jack plug is inserted into the guitar.

Under normal circumstances, a thin body like The Artistry means a rather meagre bass response. But not in this case. Mike told us that in order to enhance the guitar's bass response as much as possible, he used a special bracing system. Usually opting for a parallel brace, on this occasion he split the bracing on the bass side in order to encourage more movement of the sound board. This style of bracing has produced a very lively but even acoustic tone from the guitar.

When plugged into an amp, The Artistry serves the player well. Using the fader control to blend a guitar's electric and acoustic properties offers a very broad tonal range indeed. I found everything from traditional jazz plumminess to those all-important shimmering, bright acoustic sounds, both readily available with minimal fuss. According to Mike, when Martin was handed the finished product, it was love at first sight: "I gave it to him and he sat and played it in my workshop for three hours without stopping. I just left him to it!" And from Martin himself? "I can't think of anything I would want to change on it. I look every day but can't think of anything."

Fingernails

Anyone who has tried playing steel strung guitar with their fingernails will tell you that you can expect considerable wear and tear, especially if you're playing night after night. In order to protect my fingernails, I use a product called 'Silk Wraps' which is available from most chemists (drug stores) in the UK. Basically, this set comprises some tiny silk sheets which you stick to the nail with glue and then buff and shape as desired. It's a thing that many flamenco players do and certainly not unique to steel string players, by any means.

It's important not to cover the entire nail, as you can actually deprive them of oxygen and cause damage that way. I use the Silk Wraps - a product developed for women to strengthen their nails, incidentally - on my thumb and index fingers because these are the fingers which play on the wound strings and these tend to take the worst punishment.

As far as fingernails are concerned, everyone is different; some are born with hard nails, others with soft and there's very little we can do to make a difference once nature has made her mind up which type we get dealt.

There are vitamin B compounds you can rub into the nail root, calcium tablets to strengthen them and so on. Back in the 70s, it used to be common practice to eat gelatine in the form of 'raw' jelly (that's 'jello' in the US) a couple of times a day.

People are born with different shaped fingers, too, and this can be a crucial differential in how good or bad they are for playing guitar. Because of the shape of the fingertips, some people have to have longer nails than others, which can lead to less strength and more tearing as a result.

I'm lucky in that I have strong nails that I can leave quite short and so I don't have too much trouble in this respect.

Strings

As far as strings are concerned, I use a 12 - 52 gauge, which is considered 'medium' in jazz circles.

I'm always being asked how often I change my strings, jazz players having a reputation for leaving strings on a guitar for years, favoring the 'mellow' tone of 'worn in' strings. Surprisingly, I find that I can get through a set of acoustic strings during the first half of a Spirit of Django gig. In the band I use a plectrum and tend to be quite rough on strings as a result, but I like the sound of a new set with their sweet, high treble end. On my electric, using my fingers I tend not to be quite so despotic, but all the same, the strings need changing after almost every gig, depending where I'm playing. If it's somewhere hot like Australia or the Middle East I have to remember to take plenty of fresh sets with me.

On this point, I must add that I've recently started using 'Elixir' strings and have found I can get a lot of playing out of them because they are covered in Gortex.

Amplification

It seems to be the thing for jazz guitarists to want to travel light in terms of their amplification needs. It might be something to do with the complete lack of expectation we have in terms of road crew. Jazz musicians can't expect the kind of pampering that our rock and roll counterparts are used to and so I suppose the most easily portable amplification usually wins the day. I do have a road crew and they are very grateful to me for travelling so light!

I've used a lot of different amplifiers in my career - from Fender Twin Reverbs (before I found out about portability) to Polytones (when I did). These days, if I arrive on a solo gig, I go direct into the PA system via a DI box. My Vanden guitar's eq means that I can pretty much guarantee myself a similar sound every night and from venue to venue. At soundchecks, all I do is make sure I can hear myself through the monitor system, the eq on the PA can be virtually flat.

When I play with my group or in situations where I have to play louder, I use a small AER combo with a 10" speaker.

I don't use effects, although I did tour with a complete guitar synthesizer package back at the beginning of the 90s. I carry an 'emergency' effects box which contains a small digital reverb unit and a DI box, just incase I turn up to a venue where the sound engineer hasn't read the contract properly.

JIVE TALKING

Martin Taylor talks to David Mead about how he developed his amazing chord melody technique…

To say that Martin Taylor started playing at an early age would be something of an understatement. His first, formative steps on a remarkable career started in his pre-school years.

MT: I believe I was four. That's what I've been told, anyway. I can't really remember the very first time I played guitar because there were always guitars about the house. But I can remember my dad coming home with a ukulele – one of these Hawaiian things, red with a little palm tree on it – and I started messing around with that and driving everybody mad.

My mum asked my dad to show me some chords, to make it sound more musical and so he showed me a few and that really gave me the bug. A little later on, a friend of mine who lived across the road got a guitar and when I saw that I thought that was really what I wanted and so my dad bought me a guitar. It was made in Russia and was like a classical guitar only it had steel strings on with an absolutely horrific action. But I got this guitar and I just couldn't put it down, I just became obsessed with it and I just played all weekend and I couldn't wait to get back from school to start playing again.

DM: Your dad had an active interest in jazz, didn't he?

Yes, my dad and his friends used to be around the house and they'd put Hot Club, Eddie Lang, Carl Kress or Dick McDonough records on – a lot of the early pioneers of jazz, really – and I just loved the music. So I actually heard guitar players in the right order, I suppose, from the very beginning. I didn't hear Charlie Christian straight away, but I heard Barney Kessel, who was the next generation, then worked my way back to Charlie after that.

At that time, pop music was directed at teenagers, it wasn't really directed at young children in the way that it is now and so I didn't really have any 'fashion' ideas about music. I really liked what I heard and started to try and pick out the melodies. I can remember asking my dad what Django was doing when he played a solo and he told me that Django was improvising and to think of it as making up another melody on the spot.

DM: That's a delightful way of summing up the subject of improvisation.

MT: That's right - and as a child I found it very easy to understand. So I would play with my dad playing rhythm guitar and I would start to make up my own melodies around the chord sequence. He taught me a few chords and a few scales, although he wasn't really a guitar player, he played double bass. He just pointed me in the right direction and I went off by myself, picking it up from listening to records. There were quite a few people in those days who used to come round to play and I just used to watch them. There was a local music shop where a lot of guitar players used to get together on Saturdays and I used to go along and watch.

DM: So you've been interested in jazz from a very early age, without going through pop and rock'n'roll the way a lot of us have?

MT: Well, first of all my dad was a jazz musician also, because I was so young, I didn't have any of the peer pressure to be into a certain type of music or a certain band. That sort of thing usually happens when you get into your teens, but by the time I was in my teens, I'd been playing guitar for about ten years and I had an understanding of jazz.

DM: Did you go through the usual rigours of formally learning scales and the theory behind the music?

MT: I can remember my dad sitting me down and showing me some scales on the guitar and I got them under my fingers. I had a good ear anyway - I could hear things - and so I could hear when something was right or wrong. I really started off very crudely by playing counter melodies and just making my melody fit the sound of the chord sequence, even though I wasn't sure what it was. I'd just think, 'Well that seems to fit.' That was my launching pad and what it did more than anything was to start to unravel the mystery of the fingerboard in terms of where the notes were in relation to each other. But in terms of getting dexterity together, I just used to play, and I've always been like that; I would sooner use the time I have practicing something I'm going to use rather than doing gymnastics or exercises. So now I never play scales or anything like that.

DM: So do you think that too much emphasis is

placed up the teaching of scales?

MT: I think it's a discipline to familiarize the pupil with the fingerboard and to give them the basic dexterity needed to play the music. But I think it's a mistake to teach everything in terms of scales and modes. One of the major criticisms people make about jazz is that it just sounds like someone going up and down scales and I can always tell if someone has learned that way when I hear them play.

The route that I took in jazz was more a melodic one which stems back to the time that I thought of improvisation as playing my own melodies over a chord sequence, so I do think melodically. I don't think about scales – I know them and over the years I've learned the theory and harmony, but, to me, it's just been making music. One of the things that can happen is that you take up an instrument to make music and you become tied up with the technicalities of the instrument itself and the music is put into the background. That happens a hell of a lot in jazz, sad to say.

DM: If Django and the early jazz pioneers like Eddie Lang were an influence to you to begin with, how did your tastes develop?

MT: I came across an album by a Hammond organ player called Shirley Scott and I put it on and I heard this very tasteful, sparse guitar playing and it was Kenny Burrell. That turned my head completely and I started to look more at the American guitar players like Barney Kessell, Charlie Christian and Herb Ellis. I've always been attracted to jazz players who have a blues element – I don't believe you can play jazz without having a feel for the blues and when you hear players who don't have that there's a coldness to their playing. I think a lot of people forget that jazz is basically a more complicated form of the blues – blues with a few more chords!

But I was never one for going out and buying records and I didn't learn to read music until later on and so I didn't go out buying books. My mother used to play lots of records by Tony Bennett, Frank Sinatra and Nat King Cole and all those arrangements were by people like Nelson Riddle. I loved that orchestral sound and the way a singer could sing one note and underneath they'd change the harmony and it would change the whole feeling of that note. I would hear folk players, classical players and blues players playing very complete parts, but I

didn't hear any jazz players doing it at that time. I just wanted to be able to sit down and play something on my own. The only jazz musicians I heard who could do that were piano players, particularly Art Tatum who was such an incredible virtuoso, but there was also Bud Powell and Fats Waller and people like that. I started to try and do that sort of thing on the guitar and then I heard Joe Pass play, which I just thought was wonderful. Then I heard George Van Eps. I guess that my way of playing is more like Van Eps rather than Joe, because, although there is a lot of improvisation going on, it's all very arranged with different lines going on, whereas Joe's playing was very spontaneous. He had an incredible facility on the guitar, an incredible freedom. He could just play whatever came into his head and if he couldn't play it, he would play something that made you think he had played it.

DM: Were you able to play in jazz bands as a teenager?

MT: Not to begin with. My father had a band that used to play for weddings and village dances and things and I started playing in his band when I was eleven. I played with him until I was 14, when I joined Lennie Hastings' band. We used to work in the London area, playing jazz and we'd also do the occasional tour around the country, but the problem was that I was still at school. Pretty soon, my playing commitments started clashing with my school work and so I left school when I was 15. I joined another band which toured around the north of England and then we got a gig on the QE2 and spent a couple of years touring the Caribbean. So I went from being at school and having chalk thrown at me one minute to sitting around the QE2's aft deck pool drinking a pina colada. It was a bit of a culture shock, but I adapted to it very well.

At that time, to be in a band and just play jazz was nearly impossible, but there was still plenty of work about for musicians. I was actually doing other work, playing other types of music and backing cabaret. When I played on the QE2 there was a little bit of jazz, but it was really a little bit of everything. It was a good apprenticeship, but I knew that I didn't want to spend my life doing that. I knew I wanted to play jazz for a living, but I didn't know how I could make it happen.

During that time we did a jazz cruise on the QE2 and we supported the Count Basie

Orchestra. I got to play with the band on a couple of occasions and jam with various members after hours.

DM: I guess that, having started so young, you were always in the position where you were playing with older musicians. Do you look back on this as a form of apprenticeship?

MT: Well, yeah, because the way I got into playing professionally was a way that almost doesn't exist anymore. If you wanted to take up an instrument and start playing, then you got together with other people who played and got into a band and you played at weddings and then you got into a professional band and did summer seasons and went on the cruise ships, you played dance halls, did radio broadcasts and things like that – an old-fashioned apprenticeship. Now, if someone wants to become a jazz musician, they go to college. I don't know if college is quite as much fun, but it was good to be with musicians who had been around a long time and had seen a lot of things. I used to enjoy listening to the guys talking about the old days and things like that – the way it had all changed. And even though we're only talking about 1973/74, it was all coming to an end. Work was plentiful then; in the West End of London, you would go and play at a club and when you got fed up with that you'd go and play at another one. Bands were quite big as well; the first band I was with there were ten of us and now you see bands where there are only two people.

DM: What would you say is the greatest gift you got from playing with Stephane Grappelli?

MT: Stephane was one of the first musicians I'd played with who had the combined talent of being a great musician but being able to communicate with the audience at the same time. That fascinated me and so I sort of informally studied him, sitting next to him all those years. But that was the biggest thing I learned from him, just communicating with an audience.

DM: It must of been a fantastic thrill to play with someone who had played with Django.

MT: It was funny, because I used to make a point of thinking when I sat next to Stephane every night that I must remember all this as a special time. For a musician to be this close to someone who has been such an influence in music doesn't come along every day and many musicians go through life without ever having that experience. Stephane and Django were the first European jazz musicians who formed a group that had its own sound – a European sound. They weren't trying to emulate American musicians, they gave it their own sound and they were our musical forefathers. What I find now, after all this time has gone by, is that I go to places all over the world and people see me as part of that story – but I didn't think of that at the time. I never saw myself as being connected with the Hot Club or with Django, but because of the long period of time that I worked with Stephane and all the recordings we made, I have a link back to Django, which is something I really didn't think of at the time.

DM: When did you decide to start playing solo gigs?

MT: That started to develop really through Ike Isaacs getting me more into playing fingerstyle. Ike was a huge influence on me - not just from a playing point of view, but also his philosophy and outlook on life in general. I was getting more interested in playing the guitar as a complete instrument and Stephane would always ask me to play a tune on my own each night. Then I would accompany him with some fingerstyle playing through the evening and so that side of my playing started to develop. At the same time I had my own bands - trios, quartets and so on - and I started off playing a couple of tunes solo every night and then it got to more and more, because it was popular. Eventually, a promoter in Lincoln asked me to do a whole night on my own. I'd never played for a whole evening by myself and wasn't sure I could do it, but I went along and did it. I played the first set ok, but then ran out of material about half way through the second. So I just asked the audience if they had any requests and they started shouting out titles and it went really well. I thought, 'God, I can do a whole night on my own.' I'd had a few really bad experiences along the way with certain jazz musicians being temperamental or with drink or drug problems and so I thought that I didn't have to deal with that aggravation anymore because I could work on my own. So, as I started to perform solo, it started to create more interest in my playing outside the sphere of jazz. In some ways it seemed to connect with people more than when I was playing in straight ahead jazz groups. From there, my audience expanded and so I started to play at more general guitar events without being slotted into that box of being a jazz musician. So everything started to open up for me and I thought that I'd just carry on.

DM: How does the process of creating a chord melody version of a tune begin?

MT: Usually, it starts with the melody, but in jazz it isn't enough to have a good melody – you've got to have an interesting enough harmonic structure to mess around with. If you've got a ballad with a really fantastically strong melody, then I would keep that and re-harmonize it in the same way that an arranger would with an orchestra. But you've got to have an interesting structure to begin with.

DM: I expect a lot of people approach you wanting a formula or a method.

MT: Well, I could show you a method, but I don't always use it! I have a way of showing people how to put the three things together – bass, melody and harmony – but I don't actually think that way. After a long time of doing it, I've built up a vocabulary of how I can do things. So it becomes like the way you speak; you know the words and you know the letters that make up the words and you know the grammar. But when you speak you don't necessarily think about the individual words, letters, grammar and so on. If you did, you couldn't talk because you'd be too busy thinking about talking. So when it actually comes down to explaining the actual process of playing, that's when I get really stumped because when I'm playing I'm don't actually think about what I'm doing. When I'm playing and it's all happening and it's all coming together, I get to the point where I'm not even conscious of playing. In fact I'm not even conscious that I'm holding a guitar…

DM: It sounds like you reach some sort of meditative state.

MT: It's actually a very difficult thing to try and describe, but I'll give it a go. Scottish Travellers have a word called 'Conyach', which means 'feeling'. Some gypsies in Europe refer to it as the 'gypsy spirit'. It's something that goes back a long way and has been carried through generations of gypsy people. It's related to the aural tradition where children are taught songs by their parents and learn to sing them purely through the heart.

At a very early age I discovered that when I sat down to play the guitar, the music would somehow envelop me. I felt somehow as if I was actually 'inside' the music. Then strange things started to happen; I would feel an odd but pleasant heaviness around my body - it was something like being wrapped inside a warm sponge. The strangest thing of all is that my guitar would totally disappear. All that was left was me and the music and it felt absolutely wonderful. Somehow the guitar was able to transport me to some sort of higher plane. I've heard religious people talk about reaching this state through meditation and so on, but for me it's music. It's a very powerful thing, even as I talk about it now the hairs start stand up on the back of my neck - but this is why I play music.

DM: I guess a lot of people are going to find it very difficult to relate to basic technique.

MT: Obviously it doesn't help anyone who wants to know the process. If I had to summarize, I would say that I know all the things I need to know to put the whole thing together, but now I've got them, I don't need them any more.

DM: So the various techniques involved are part of your sub-conscious, almost reflex actions?

MT: That's about it, yeah. The thing I tell people about the bass, chords and melody thing is that I think more of the melody and bassline – I keep those in my mind and pick out harmony in the middle. But I don't always do that; if somebody wants some help in getting into that style of playing, then I would say that is your starting point. The last thing I want to do is to get esoteric about talking about it because that doesn't help anyone or answer any questions. It's just that I've played so much over such a long period of time and dedicated everything I do to that, it's just a part of me. Even if I sit in my front room and play, I pick the guitar up, I'm absorbed in the music. If I'm having a bad night, it's not because I'm not playing well, because one of the things about playing a lot and getting to a certain level is that you don't have real extremes – you don't drop below a certain level. If I'm playing slightly under, then it feels to me like I'm really playing badly, but if I hear a recording, it's actually all right. But the difference to me is huge. One of the ways that I judge that is that I'm suddenly very aware of playing a guitar – I've got this bloody great piece of wood and I'm trying to get some music out of it and I'm thinking about playing the guitar, which is not what I do. I play the guitar.

DM: And, I would guess, you've long since dealt with the horrors associated with playing in public?

MT: Oh yeah. But I know some fantastic players who can't perform in front of an audience – it's not for everyone. It's such a fantastically unnatural environment to be in. I travel all over the world, playing guitar in front of people on my own. I travel thousands of miles, check into a hotel, try to grab something to eat, go to a strange venue, do a soundcheck, come off, and then walk back out on stage in front of all these people who are expecting at least one hundred percent. You stand in the middle of the stage under lights, become hot, the guitar goes out of tune, you've got foldback which means you're not hearing the true sound of the instrument. You've got all these things stacked against you, but for me, I thrive on it; it actually makes me play better.

DM: How do see your style continuing to develop in the future?

MT: For me, where playing solo guitar is concerned, I don't think of myself getting better on the guitar, being able to play more or anything like that, I just think in terms of musical freedom – actually being able to play the ideas that I have. That doesn't mean trying to play things that are complicated or fast – in fact I don't play as much as you think I play. When my solos are transcribed, there isn't as much going on as you think it's just that I try to give the impression that there's more happening. It's actually breaking everything down to the bare bones, because a guitar player has to suggest things are happening in his playing which fall beyond the scope of the instrument. I think all guitar players will know what I mean when I say that you have all these ideas, but somewhere between your head and your fingers, there's a communication breakdown. That's a thing which has to be overcome somewhere along the way.

DAVID MEAD

David Mead has played on radio, TV, in bars and clubs all across the UK. A private teacher for longer than he cares to remember, he embarked upon a career in journalism around 1992 when he joined the staff of UK's prestigious *Guitarist* magazine, working his way up to editor three years later. From there, he joined *Guitar Techniques* magazine as editor, a post he held for six and a half years before leaving to pursue a career as a writer and musician.

He remains fully active in the field of guitar education, holding the post of director and course leader of the International Guitar Festival in Bath, UK, taking part in seminars all over the country and writing a monthly column on sight reading for Guitar Techniques magazine.

David has written many guitar tutors, among them the best-selling "Ten Minute Guitar Workout," "100 Guitar Tips" and "100 Acoustic Guitar Tips." He has also co-written Martin Taylor's autobiography, "Kiss and Tell," and edited Doug Sundling's definitive "Ultimate Doors Companion." All titles are available from Sanctuary Publishing, London, UK.

© Carol Farnworth

www.davidmead.net
email - info@davidmead.net

MARTIN TAYLOR MBE

"There is a touch of genius in Martin Taylor's playing."

CLASSICAL GUITAR MAGAZINE

The virtuoso guitarist Martin Taylor first came to prominence in the late 1970's through his collaborations with the jazz violin legend Stephane Grappelli, and now tours the world's concert halls with his dazzling live performances.

He began playing at the age of four when his father, jazz bassist Buck Taylor, gave him a small acoustic guitar as a present. A totally self taught guitarist, he learned to play by listening to his father's records and trying to imitate what he heard. Seven years later he was playing in local bands and gained the respect and admiration of professional musicians who were amazed by the young boy they called "The Guitar Wizard."

Although inspired initially by the Gypsy guitarist Django Reinhardt, it was to be piano players, most notably Art Tatum, that caught his imagination and set him on the path of developing his own individual style of solo playing.

In 1978 he made his debut album *Taylor Made* for Wave Records and the following year received a call from Stephane Grappelli inviting him to play on a series of concerts in France. Shortly after those concerts he joined Stephane on a coast-to-coast tour of the U.S, including New York's Carnegie Hall and the Hollywood Bowl. It was the beginning of an eleven year collaboration which took in numerous world tours, and over 20 albums including recordings with Michel Legrand, Peggy Lee, Yehudi Menuhin, Nelson Riddle and several film soundtracks including the Louis Malle movie *Milou en Mai* and *Dirty Rotten Scoundrels* starring Steve Martin and Michael Caine.

Alongside his work with Grappelli, he was also pursuing his own solo career and in 1987 had great commercial success in America with his Los Angeles recorded album *Sarabanda.*

In 1993 he made his first solo album for Linn Records *Artistry,* which topped the UK jazz charts for six weeks and made him the biggest selling British jazz artist in the UK.

The following year he formed his group "Spirit of Django," and their first recording for Linn Records also proved to be a best selling jazz album and was nominated best album in the British Jazz Awards and Martin was voted best guitarist for the seventh time in a row.

Even people who are not familiar with Martin's work will have heard him many times with his version of Robert Palmer's *Johnny and Mary,* which was used on the famous cult TV ads with "Nicole-Papa" for the Renault Clio.

In 1999 he signed a recording contract with Sony Jazz, making two critically acclaimed albums *Kiss and Tell* and *Nitelife.*

He has also collaborated with many musicians outside of jazz including Yes guitarist Steve Howe and country guitar legend Chet Atkins. He was also featured on the Prefab Sprout album *Andromeda Heights,* and has recorded with George Harrison, Eric Clapton, Chris Rea, and ex-Rolling Stone Bill Wyman.

In 1998 he founded the Kirkmichael International Guitar Festival in his home village in Scotland, which has now become one of the biggest guitar festivals in the world. He also founded Guitars For Schools, which promotes the teaching of guitars in primary schools. Through his work he has raised money to pay for guitars and tuition for hundreds of school children throughout South West Scotland.

Over the years he has received many awards and honours including The Freedom of the City of London, the Gold Badge Of Merit from the British Academy of Composers and Songwriters, and was made an Honorary Doctor of the University of Paisley, Scotland in celebration of 25 years in music.

In 2002, on the recommendation of the British Prime Minister Tony Blair, Martin was made a Member of the Order of the British Empire (MBE) for Services to Jazz Music, in the Queen's Jubilee Birthday Honours List, making him the first jazz guitarist ever to receive an honour from the Queen. His autobiography for Sanctuary Publishing "Kiss and Tell" is available worldwide.

His latest album "SOLO" is available on P3 Music www.p3music.com

"Europe's finest guitarist" – Jazz Times New York

"THE acoustic guitarist of his generation" - Acoustic Guitar Magazine

"A great artist" – Stephane Grappelli

"On of the greatest and most impressive guitarists in the world today. I just love his playing!" - Chet Atkins

"Martin Taylor's solo playing is absolutely inspiring and amazing"
– Pat Metheny

www.martintaylor.com

Photo Credit: Chris Lopez